A. S. Hale

PREACHING WITH AUTHORITY

THE LYMAN BEECHER LECTURES ON PREACHING
DELIVERED AT YALE IN APRIL, 1929

BY

EDWIN DuBOSE MOUZON

ONE OF THE BISHOPS OF THE METHODIST
EPISCOPAL CHURCH, SOUTH

DOUBLEDAY, DORAN & COMPANY, INC.

GARDEN CITY, NEW YORK

1929

TO

MY WIFE

MARY PEARL

A TRUE FRIEND AND HELPFUL COMPANION

PREACHING WITH AUTHORITY

PREFACE

I AM under obligation to the Rev. Plato T. Durham, A.B., B.D., D.D., Professor of Church History in Candler School of Theology, Emory University, Atlanta, Georgia, and to the Rev. Gilbert T. Rowe, A.B., S.T.D., Litt.D., D.D., Professor of Christian Doctrine in the School of Religion, Duke University, Durham, North Carolina, who were guests in my home for a day and a night and listened patiently to the reading of these lectures. I am also under obligation to President Henry N. Snyder, A.M., D.Litt., LL.D., of Wofford College, Spartanburg, South Carolina, who kindly read the manuscript before these pages went to the press. These friends made valuable suggestions. For the suggestion, in the latter part of Lecture II, that one wing of the liberal movement in the modern Church has drifted far from the liberalism of the New Testament Church, the Reformation, and the Evangelical Revival, I am indebted to the Rev. H. B. Trimble, M.A., B.D., D.D., Pastor of Central Methodist Church, Asheville, North Carolina. Besides, I am indebted to the Rev. G. Ray Jordan, M.A., B.D., Pastor of Dilworth Methodist Church, Charlotte, N.C., who was good enough to read the proof.

I wish to express to the publishers who freely and gladly granted me the privilege of making quotations from their publications my sincere appreciation of their courtesy: to Charles Scribner's Sons for quotations from Gwatkin's *The Knowledge of God* and Edward's *Religious Experience;* to the Macmillan Company for quotations from Montague's *Ways of Knowing* and from Temple's *Christ the Way;* to Harper & Brothers for a quotation from Dodd's *The Authority of the Bible;* to Doubleday, Doran & Company for quotations from Moffatt's *Everyman's Life of Jesus* and from Gordon's *Prophets of the Old Testament;* to Houghton Mifflin Company for short extracts from Allen's *The Continuity of Christian Thought;* and to D. Appleton & Company for a passage from Campbell's *A Spiritual Pilgrimage.* The Bible text used in this book, with the exception of the chapter quoted in the Personal Foreword, is taken from the American Standard Edition of the Revised Bible, copyright, 1901, by Thomas Nelson & Sons, and is used by permission.

I desire also to give expression to my deep appreciation of the many courtesies extended me by Dean Luther A. Weigle of the Divinity School of Yale University while I was visiting in New Haven and giving these lectures. And I shall not forget the delightful association I had with members of the faculty and with earnest-minded students.

CONTENTS

PERSONAL FOREWORD

MY CERTIFICATE of license to preach bears the date November 20, 1888. It is signed by the Rev. Thos. G. Herbert, Presiding Elder, and A. H. Kirby, Secretary of the Quarterly Conference of Central Methodist Church, Spartanburg, South Carolina. My father, Samuel Cogswell Mouzon, was a modest layman. He had, during all the period of my childhood and youth, regularly conducted family worship morning and evening, reading one of the Psalms in the morning and a lesson from the New Testament in the evening. The evening I was going up for my examination he turned aside from the regular course of his reading and read instead the second chapter of Second Timothy. He offered no explanation for so doing and he made no comment. But the reading of that scripture made on my mind a profound impression. I am printing that lesson here with the hope that the message it conveyed to me many years ago may be conveyed to such young men as may read these lectures.

Thou, therefore, my son, be strong in the grace that is in Christ Jesus.

And the things that thou hast heard of me among many witnesses, the same commit thou to faithful men, who shall be able to teach others also.

Thou therefore endure hardness, as a good soldier of Jesus Christ.

No man that warreth entangleth himself with the affairs of this life; that he may please him that hath chosen him to be a soldier.

And if a man also strive for masteries, yet is he not crowned, except he strive lawfully.

The husbandman that laboureth must be first partaker of the fruits.

Consider what I say; and the Lord give thee understanding in all things.

Remember that Jesus Christ of the seed of David was raised from the dead according to my gospel:

Wherein I suffer trouble, as an evil doer, even unto bonds; but the word of God is not bound.

Therefore I endure all things for the elect's sakes, that they may also obtain the salvation which is in Christ Jesus with eternal glory.

It is a faithful saying: For if we be dead with him, we shall also live with him:

If we suffer, we shall also reign with him: if we deny him, he also will deny us:

If we believe not, yet he abideth faithful: he cannot deny himself.

Of these things put them in remembrance, charging them before the Lord that they strive not about words to no profit, but to the subverting of the hearers.

Study to show thyself approved unto God, a workman that needeth not to be ashamed, rightly dividing the word of truth.

But shun profane and vain babblings: for they will increase unto more ungodliness.

And their word will eat as doth a canker: of whom is Hymenæus and Philetus;

Who concerning the truth have erred, saying that the resurrection is past already; and overthrow the faith of some.

Nevertheless the foundation of God standeth sure, having this seal, The Lord knoweth them that are his. And, Let every one that nameth the name of Christ depart from iniquity.

But in a great house there are not only vessels of gold and

of silver, but also of wood and of earth; and some to honour, and some to dishonour.

If a man therefore purge himself from these, he shall be a vessel unto honour, sanctified, and meet for the master's use, and prepared unto every good work.

Flee also youthful lusts: but follow righteousness, faith, charity, peace, with them that call on the Lord out of a pure heart.

But foolish and unlearned questions avoid, knowing that they do gender strifes.

And the servant of the Lord must not strive; but be gentle unto all men, apt to teach, patient.

In meekness instructing those that oppose themselves; if God peradventure will give them repentance to the acknowledging of the truth;

And that they may recover themselves out of the snare of the devil, who are taken captive by him at his will.

EDWIN DuBOSE MOUZON.

Charlotte, North Carolina.

I

AUTHORITY AND AUTHORITIES

"He taught them as having authority and not as the scribes."
—MARK 1 : 22.

I

AUTHORITY AND AUTHORITIES

SOME time since I received a letter from a young man just about to enter the ministry in which he submitted a most vital question. This is what he asked: "The old authorities are gone. What are we to do? Where is any new authority?" I wrote him in the following language: " 'When the half-gods go, then the whole-gods come.' If the things that can be shaken have been shaken, it is in order that the things that cannot be shaken may remain."

We recognize at the very beginning of this series of lectures that we are living in the midst of times of profound interest in religion. The heart hungers for reality; the mind is in search of the ultimate. Also we live in the midst of widespread theological unrest and upheaval. In all this there is much that is unmixed good; there is also much that is evil. If asked the reason for the present situation we should have to reply that the explanation is not altogether simple. There are many reasons for it.

We should say that it is in part occasioned by a generally prevalent spirit of rebellion against the established order of things. It is what the Germans would call the *zeitgeist,* the very spirit of the times. Men are in opposition to authority everywhere. Old established governments have been overturned and new experiments in government put in their stead. Even the old morality has been called in question, and our innovators are trying to work out a new morality on a purely naturalistic basis. Especially are the young trying out new ways and seeking out new foundations. The present theological unrest is one phase of what we call "the revolt of youth."

A second explanation will come somewhat nearer to the heart of the matter. In the year 1901 W. Robertson Nicoll wrote to James Denney: "I am sure that when the people get to understand what is involved in the critical view of the New Testament, they will be deeply moved, some to complete rejection of Christianity, and many to a fierce unreasoning bigotry." And this is precisely what has happened. On the one hand, the critics have advanced theories that have been an offense to the common sense of the rank and file of Christians, and on the other hand men with a superficial knowledge of science have taken such extreme positions that now Nicoll's prophecy is in the midst of its fulfillment— some people have been moved to a complete rejection of Christianity and many to a fierce unreasoning bigotry, while between the two are many others in a state of great perplexity.

But we offer a third reason for the present state of theological upheaval. The profound and underlying reason for the conflict now seen in the religious world traces back to two diametrically opposed views of the essential nature of religion. With some religion is static, fixed, finished, and finite—a thing for definition and codification, to be handed down from antiquity and enforced by external authority. With others religion is dynamic, living, growing, and infinite—a matter for faith and experience, a thing to be kept alive by holy living and passed on to others by the inward authority of the Spirit of God speaking directly to the spirit of man. Here is the watershed of all religious systems, of all systems of theology in all lands and all ages. Here they divide and part company. Equally honest and earnest men are to be found on the one side as on the other. The two systems correspond to two different types of mind.

Permit me now in a few words to make my own position clear before we proceed further. I believe in a universe that is alive. I believe in the living God. I believe in a God who is in the midst of things. I do not believe in a God who stands on the outside of things and occasionally breaks in—as in the creation of life, the creation of man, the giving of the law through Moses, and the coming of Christ. But never is all of God seen in nature or in history; God is transcendent as well as immanent. God is more fully seen in a flower than in a stone; he is more fully revealed in a song-bird than in a violet; he is more fully disclosed in man than in any of the lower animals. He is seen supremely in Jesus Christ. And God is always near. In him we live and move and have our being. God is always at work in all things—in nature, in history, and in the life of the world to-day as truly as when life was first created or man was made.

At this very point there emerges a truth that separates asunder, as far as the poles, the two views of religion mentioned above. And this is the truth that lies basal in all truly spiritual religion, the truth that God made man in his own image and after his own likeness. God and man are not unlike and disparate; God and man are akin. They are alike as father and child. There is a spark of the divine shining in all men. There is that within man which responds to the approach of God. There is an inner ear that is able to hear the divine voice. The human child knows when the divine Father calls. There is an inward light that kindles up brightly when the light of God's truth shines forth. And we need not fear to trust the authority of this inward light. If we follow on to know the Lord he will make himself more and more fully known. Nor do we need anything more than this—only this and all that this implies.

Oman, in his *Vision and Authority,* has a chapter entitled, "The Authority of the Optic Nerve." At first thought it seems surprising that our entire knowledge of things seen should rest on the slender authority of the optic nerve, but so it is. If the optic nerve should be cut in two, then we should be plunged into total darkness. If the optic nerve be diseased, then with great pain do we see at all. If the optic nerve be damaged, then do we see a blurred world. But as a matter of fact, the entire world as seen rests on the authority of so delicate an instrument of knowledge. For us the chaste beauty of the early morning, the glory of sunset skies, the splendor of the noontide—all depend upon a sound organ of sight. And in like manner there is a most delicate organ of spiritual vision, and it was with reference to this that Jesus said: "If the light that is in you be darkness, how great is that darkness."

"I have a little inward light, which still
  All tenderly I keep, and ever will.
  I think it never wholly dies away;
  But oft it seems as if it could not stay,
  And I do strive to keep it if I may.

. . . . . .

"O God! O Father! hear thy child who cries!
  Who would not quench the flame; who would not dare
  To let it dwindle in a sinful air;
  Who does feel how all-precious such a prize,
  And yet, alas! is feeble and not wise."[1]

The essential difference, then, between the two views of religion as mentioned above is that one represents the religion that rests upon outward authorities and the other represents the religion that depends

---

[1] Henry Septimus Sutton.

on the authority of spiritual vision, the authority of the voice of God sounding in the souls of men. We proceed now to show how this distinction runs through the entire history of religion.

I

As soon as one opens the Old Testament and begins to read it carefully one sees therein two types of writing, the priestly and the prophetic.

For the student of the Old Testament this is his introduction to the historic study of the Bible. Not until this has been pointed out is he able intelligently to go on. The priestly writers are the conservatives and reactionaries. They are interested in genealogies and chronicles. They are careful about ritual. They codify the laws. They treasure up the traditions. On the other side are the prophetic writers. They are the innovators. They are the reformers. They do startling things. They listen for the voice of God not alone in the records of the past, but in the stillness and silence of their own souls. They are God's spokesmen; they speak in the name of God and for God. They see how God is moving in the events of the present. They urge that men move along with God. What sounds as but a faint whisper in other souls sounds as a loud voice in their hearts. Said Amos: "The lion hath roared: who will not fear? The Lord hath spoken, who can but prophesy?" They care but little for codified laws and elaborated ritual. They cry, "Behold, to obey is better than sacrifice, and to hearken than the fat of lambs." In the true prophetic spirit the Psalmist enunciated the spiritual principle, "Thou delightest not in sacrifice, else would I give it: thou hast no pleasure in burnt offering. The sacrifices of God are a broken spirit; a broken and a contrite heart, O God, thou wilt not despise." But a later priestly writer was not willing to let the Fifty-first Psalm end that way, and added the amendment, "Do good in thy good pleasure unto Zion: Build thou the walls of Jerusalem. Then wilt thou delight in the sacrifices of righteousness, in burnt offering and whole burnt offering: Then will they offer bullocks upon thine altar."

The most interesting and illuminating instance in the Old Testament of this conflict of ideals, this contrast between the religion of authority and the religion of the spirit, may be seen during the reign of King Josiah in the Eighth Century B. C. While important work of repair was going on in the temple a surprising discovery was made. The high priest announced to Shaphan the scribe that he had found the Book of the Law in the temple. When the King learned the contents of the book he was alarmed over the manner in which the law had been violated and over the direful threats of punishment contained therein. Straightway he took steps to bring the practices of the people into harmony with the Book of Deuteronomy. It was a thoroughgoing reform, and nothing, let it be noted, is here said in discount of the deep-seated and far-reaching consequences of Josiah's reform. Its influences were felt in all subsequent history of the Jewish people. Deuteronomy has much of the prophetic spirit in it. It is a beautiful book. Jesus and Paul read the Book of Deuteronomy. But the religion of the Book of Deuteronomy is, in the main, the religion of external authority. It is definitely a state religion. The nation became the Church and the Church the nation. Religion was henceforth definitely legalistic; Judah became for the first time the people of the Law.

Deuteronomy, as George Adam Smith points out, has three cardinal doctrines: the One God, the One Altar, the One People. The monotheism of the book is moral and warmly spiritual. There is one God and he must be loved with all the heart and mind and soul and strength. There is to be only one altar. Various shrines in different places had led gradually to shameless idolatry. Now all sacrifices must be offered upon the one altar at the capital of the nation. And Israel is to be the one people. Next to pride in the one God comes pride in the nation. The Book of Deuteronomy presents "as comprehensive a system of national religion as the world has ever known."

The reading of the book stirred to the depths the people as well as the King, and presently a great religious revival was inaugurated. All the high places were swept away, a ban was placed on private sacrifices, and all offerings were restricted to the temple in Jerusalem. "A sharp distinction was thereby drawn between the laity and the priests, between secular and holy things. Religion henceforth became something formal, above and apart, rather than in all which concerned the nation or individual."[2] For the time being all seemed to go well. Vast changes had passed over the whole outward look of things. But as a matter of fact, the reform had been almost wholly outward rather than inward, and religion having become national and having been centralized in Jerusalem, became less personal and intimate and spiritual. As A. B. Davidson says, "Pharisaism and Deuteronomy came into the world on the same day."

Now the period of Josiah is also the period of Jeremiah. Both men were interested in reform. But Josiah and Jeremiah are wide apart in the kind of reform that concerned them most. The sort of reform that Jeremiah strove to bring about was not formal, legal, and ritualistic, but spiritual, intimate, and inward. The "covenant" Jeremiah was most interested in was not a covenant that codified ancient laws and was written down in a book. It was rather a covenant between the individual and his God, open to all men everywhere, and having spiritual and final authority. Such a covenant, Jeremiah saw plainly, would, if allowed to have its way, change the nation by remaking individuals, would reform the outward order by re-forming the heart and life. In all the literature of religion there are not to be found any nobler words, words of deeper spiritual insight, than

---

[2]Kent, *A History of the Hebrew People*, p. 180, "The Divided Kingdom."

the words of Jeremiah wherein he advocates the sort of reform that will abide:

"Behold, the days come, saith Jehovah, that I will make a new covenant with the house of Israel and with the house of Judah: not according to the covenant that I made with their fathers in the day that I took them by the hand to bring them out of the land of Egypt; which my covenant they brake, although I was a husband unto them, saith Jehovah. But this is the covenant that I will make with the house of Israel after those days, saith Jehovah: I will put my law in their inward parts, and in their heart will I write it; and I will be their God and they shall be my people. And they shall teach no more every man his neighbor, and every man his brother, saying, Know Jehovah; for they shall all know me from the least of them unto the greatest of them, saith Jehovah: for I will forgive their iniquity, and their sin will I remember no more."[3]

And let us pause here long enough to mention the fact that the very words, "the new convenant," "the New Testament," come to us in direct spiritual descent from Jeremiah. The Christianity of Jesus and Paul and John cannot be essentially different in spirit from the religion of Jeremiah. We at the present time, therefore, should be careful to see to it that we are in fact, and not in name only, "Ministers of a new covenant; not of the letter, but of the spirit; for the letter killeth, but the spirit giveth life."

---

[3] Jeremiah 31: 31-34.

II

Passing now to the New Testament period, we see these two types of religion, these two ways of approaching the entire matter of authority in religion, in the sharpest sort of conflict.

See how this is illustrated both in Jesus and in Paul.

The preaching of Jesus startled the scribes and Pharisees. It was revolutionary. It was observed at once that "he taught as one having authority, and not as the scribes." The point is exactly this: the scribes had *authorities* a plenty behind them, but they had no spiritual authority. On the other hand, Jesus cared little for ancient authorities; he spoke with authority, direct, personal, divine.

At the time of Christ the voice of the prophet had long been silent, save only the voice of John the Baptist which had begun to wake men from their slumber in such a way as to remind them of Elijah and Jeremiah. In Judaism the scribe had taken the place of the prophet. The scribe had become the divine aristocrat among the vulgar herd of rude and profane "country people" who "know not the law" and are "cursed." More than that, the scribe had become the ultimate authority on all questions of faith and practice. He was "the exegete of the laws," the "teacher of the law," and along with the "chief priests" and "elders," a judge in the ecclesiastical tribunals whether in the capital or in the provinces. Says Edersheim, "Such was the respect paid to their sayings, that they were to be absolutely believed, even if they were to declare that to be at the right hand which was at the left, or *vice versa*."

The essential fault of their system, the entire system of Judaism, was that it was deistic. Their God was not immanent but wholly transcendent—not in the midst of things, the ground and source of all that is, but outside of all things and distant from men. Once God had done something; now he was idle. Once God had spoken; now he was silent. His words, written down in their Sacred Scriptures and interpreted in the traditions of the elders, had been delivered as a sacred deposit into the keeping of the scribes, who alone now had the right to interpret them. Their universe was not dynamic, it was static. Their world was not alive, it was dead—frozen.

No wonder Jesus startled people! He spoke with authority, not as one who had to bolster up what he said by quoting ancient and superior authorities. Jesus was alive and his universe was alive. Said he, "My father worketh even until now and I work." And observe carefully how Jesus taught: "Ye have heard that it was said to them of old time, Thou shalt not kill—But I say unto you, Thou shalt not harbor anger nor contempt." "Ye have heard that it was said to them of old time, Thou shalt not commit adultery—But I say unto you that adultery traces back to the lustful heart." "Ye have heard that it was said, Thou shalt not swear falsely—But I say unto you, Let your speech be a simple Yes or No."

"Ye have heard that it was said, An eye for an eye and a tooth for a tooth—But I say unto you, Resist not the evil man, but rather return good for evil." "Ye have heard that it was said to them of old time, Thou shalt love thy neighbor and hate thine enemy—But I say unto you, Love your enemies." "Ye, therefore, shall be perfect, as your heavenly Father is perfect."

That is the way Jesus put it. And he left it there, not buttressing it up with external authority but simply affirming, "I say unto you," and trusting the truth to find its native home in the human heart.

And why should it ever be supposed necessary to buttress the truth with something other than the truth and different from it in order to get people to believe the truth? There is no truth greater than the truth. We should just as wisely seek to find something superior to light to enable us to be sure that the light is shining, or superior to heat, to convince us that there is warmth in the sunshine.

Jesus set himself squarely against everything characteristic of Pharisaism. In the twenty-third chapter of Matthew the entire system is brought to the judgment bar. Seven times in that chapter we have it: "Woe unto you, scribes and Pharisees, hypocrites!" But even so his heart was breaking, and he cries: "O Jerusalem, Jerusalem, that killeth the prophets, and stoneth them that are sent unto her! how often would I have gathered thy children together, even as a hen gathereth her chickens under her wings, and you would not!"

And in contrast with Pharisaism see how inward and spiritual the religion of Jesus is: "The kingdom of heaven is within you." "Blessed are the pure in heart for they shall see God." "The Sabbath was made for man and not man for the Sabbath"; that is to say, institutions exist for men, not men for institutions. "Perceive ye not, that whatsoever from without goeth into a man, it cannot defile him. . . . This he said, making all meats clean." "Believe me, the hour cometh, when neither in this mountain, nor in Jerusalem, shall ye worship the Father . . . but when the true worshippers shall worship the Father in spirit and in truth."

It was precisely over these two divergent views of religion that the great battle raged in New Testament times. It was the ever-recurrent struggle between the spiritual and the legalistic. Peter made a brave beginning in the house of the gentile Cornelius. But even Peter's vision of the sheet let down by the four corners from heaven and filled with all manner of beasts ceremonially unclean and the accompanying command, "Rise, Peter, kill and eat," did not permanently change his Jewish outlook. It was Paul, the converted Pharisee, who saved the day for the religion of the spirit. The persistence of some of Peter's earlier prejudices calls to mind an amusing thrust that Jesus made at the scribes: "And he said unto them, therefore, every *scribe* who hath been made a disciple unto the kingdom of heaven is like unto a man that is a householder, who bringeth forth out of his treasure things new and *old."* *"Old,"* it will be observed as well as "new." Something of the scribe still remains in the scribe after his conversion and he continues to count the *old* as being in his *treasure,* whereas Jesus came to make all things new. But Paul, as did his Master, laid the ax at the root of the tree. He is the great protagonist of freedom among the writers of the New Testament. The Epistle to the Galatians is the Magna Charta of New Testament religion. The apostle begins this letter with the sure note of spiritual authority: "Paul, an apostle (not from men, neither through man, but through Jesus Christ, and God the Father, who raised him from the dead)."There and there alone was the source of his authority. And the keynote of the Galatian letter, and of the religion of the New Testament, is to be found in these memorable words: "For freedom did Christ set us free: stand fast, therefore, and be not entangled again in a yoke of bondage." For no one book in the New Testament should we be more grateful than for this Epistle to the Galatians. In every period of reaction it has called men back to liberty and progress. Everybody knows how Martin Luther rejoiced in this book. In his own intimate and human way he said, "The Epistle to the Galatians is my epistle. I have betrothed myself to it. It is my wife."

And at the present time, when even in evangelical

circles literalism and dogmatism are striving to gain the mastery, we need once more to urge that the true evangel is a gospel of liberty.

III

The line of cleavage, which we have seen running through the Old Testament and the New, cuts all the way down through the history of the Church.

A careful reading of history makes this perfectly evident. In the early days of the Church two types of mind were in conflict, two methods of approach to religion struggled for the mastery, the Greek on the one hand and the Latin on the other. In the breaking up of the Eastern Empire Greek culture also collapsed and with it failed the Greek method of approaching theological questions. Greek thought was the ripe fruit of centuries of culture. The Greek mind had the instinct for reality. I do not doubt that if the situation had been different, that if the West had collapsed, and the East had been able to live through the vast changes of the time, that if we modern men had inherited our theology from Clement and Athanasius rather than from Tertullian and Augustine, our adjustment to the new world of knowledge opened during recent years by scientists, philosophers, and scholars would have been natural and easy and reassuring. For the Greek theologians brought out into clear light the implications of John's great saying: "In the beginning was the Word and the Word was with God and the Word was God. . . . And the Word became flesh and dwelt among us (and we beheld his glory, glory as of the only begotten of the Father), full of grace and truth."

But the Latin mind had no instinct for philosophy. It was almost wholly practical. It had a genius for organization and government. The Roman Church easily fitted itself into the governmental forms of the dying Roman Empire, and is indeed the continuation of that empire. "The Latin Church had no more aptitude for theology than the Latin people had for philosophy throughout their history. . . . A deep and instinctive aversion to all speculative thought, a desire for a definite faith firmly grounded on tradition as the only stable basis, a faith that could be as exactly formulated as a code of law, the slightest variation from which could be easily detected and exposed—such was the characteristic, the ideal, and the ambition of the Latin Church in the Second and Third centuries, and such they have remained throughout her entire career."[4]

Tertullian had been a Roman lawyer, and his legal mind is seen in his defense of the faith set forth in his famous "Prescription of Heresy." According to Tertullian the faith is the property of the Church, which the Church must protect and defend against all comers. Christianity can have nothing to do with philosophy. Heresy is nothing but self-will. "Away with all efforts to produce a mottled Christianity of Stoic, Platonic, and dialectic composition." There is

---

[4] Allen, *Continuity of Christian Thought*, p. 114.

no need of seeking after Truth; the Church has it in her possession. It is to be found only in the Church, and when once found all inquiry should cease.

The great name, however, in the Latin Church is, of course, the name of Augustine, and his shadow still falls athwart our path. In his earlier years he had come strongly under the influence of Greek thought. His *Confessions* is a book of devotions for Protestants as well as for Catholics. But Augustine became of necessity an administrator and at a time when only a strong hand could save the Church from being overwhelmed in the general overthrow. And as Allen says, "the necessities of ecclesiastical administration in the see of Hippo had revolutionized his intellectual methods and led him to economize the truth in the interest of the Church." Thus it came about that Augustine made it his life work "to adjust special institutions and even humanity itself to the claims of a hierarchy divinely appointed to teach and rule the world."[5]

All the way down through Christian history the two differing views of God and the two contradictory views of human nature have determined men's attitude toward things theological and ecclesiastical. If I may borrow a suggestive classification, one view is seen in the *disciplinarian* and the other view is seen in the *mystic*. To the disciplinarian, Christ is the bread of life which came down from heaven in such a year of Cæsar Augustus; to the mystic he is also the

---

[5]Allen, *Continuity of Christian Thought*, pp. 148, 149, 150.

bread of life which is ever coming down and ever giving his life for the whole world. A quotation from Gwatkin will state succinctly and set forth clearly the significance and the implications of these two views: "The one looks back to the majestic memory of a revelation given once for all, a faith delivered once for all, a visible Church set up once for all, with a sacred trust of laws and ordinances to be maintained against a wicked world. He is the materialist of Christian thought, as firmly convinced as any unbeliever that the Gospel works contrary to nature and reason. So he looks for its evidence in breaches of natural order, finds the grace of heaven in sacraments and mysteries outside the domain of reason, and waits for salvation in the horrors of the Lord's return, when he shall overthrow like Sodom a world beyond his power fully to redeem. The other lives by a growing revelation and a growing knowledge of an ever-living Person whose kingdom ruleth over all, but only by the appeal of love divine to the image of God in man. He is the idealist of Christian thought, who sees in reason and Nature no mirage of hellish magic, but shadows of the eternal truth incarnate in the Son of Man. So he looks for the evidence of the Gospel in its revelation of this world's true estate and order, sees the grace of heaven in every work that is done on the wide earth for love and duty, and looks for life eternal here and now, not simply as the future issue of some far-off divine catastrophe."[6]

[6]*The Knowledge of God*, Vol. ii, pp. 57–58.

IV

It is here at this great watershed that the two systems, Catholicism and Protestantism, part company and go on each in its own way. Catholicism relies upon authorities set up and obedience enforced from without. Protestantism is true to herself only when she relies upon the authority that comes from God alone.

At the close of the Fifteenth Century the religion of external authority was everywhere dominant and Catholicism seemed secure in its absolute control of the intellect and conscience and life of men. However, it was only a time of silence before a great awakening. Indeed, God had never left the truth entirely without witnesses. All along through the so-called Dark Ages there had been holy men and significant movements that indicated that the lamp of truth had not entirely gone out. There had been John the Scot in the Ninth Century who taught that "there are as many unveilings of God as there are saintly souls." There had been Francis of Assisi in the Thirteenth Century, who came at a time when genuine Christianity was almost extinct and brought back religion to the common people, making it a thing of joy and gladness. And at the beginning of the Fourteenth Century there had been Meister Eckhart, who dropped his plummet deep into the mysteries of religion and whom the Pope condemned as having "wished to know more than he should." And in the same century lived John Tauler, who insisted that "the man who truly experiences the pure presence of God in his own soul knows well that there can be no doubt that there is an entrance into union of the created spirit with the uncreated spirit of God." The Waldenses, the Friends of God, the Brethren of the Common Life, and many other groups of mystics had found their way to the Father in spite of all the bars erected by the Church between the individual and his God. And there, too, had been England's greatest religious prophet, Wycliffe, "the morning star of the Reformation," who stands among the foremost prophets of the Christian Church.[7] All these had found where the ground of Christian certitude lies, namely, in the soul's experience of communion with God.

But it was, of course, Martin Luther who, coming in the fullness of time, taught that salvation is the free gift of God, not to be bought with money nor purchased through merit; who taught that the perfect Christian life is not to be found in monasticism, but in daily holy living and in love of our neighbors; who taught the priesthood of all believers—that all men may without the intermediation of another have direct access to the Father; who opened the Bible and gave it to the common people that therein they might hear sounding the "word of God"; who overturned the false authorities of Catholicism and showed how neither Pope nor Councils had unerring authority,

[7] For these references see Jones, *Studies in Mystical Religion.*

but only the Gospel, the power and truth of which the soul inwardly knows.

Over against this definitely spiritual view of the essence and authority of religion is set the Catholic view, the same in principle whether found in the Anglican, the Greek, or the Roman Church.

Here, by way of illustration, is a scholarly volume written by Dr. Charles Harris of the Church of England under the title, *Creeds or No Creeds?* in which the position is strongly maintained that the ultimate ground of authority is in the Church, and that in the Catholic Creeds infallible and final interpretation of the Christian faith is to be found. Jesus, according to the Fourth Gospel, had given to his disciples the promise of "the Spirit of truth" to "guide into all truth." The author of *Creeds or No Creeds?* denies that this was a promise to individual apostles and *"still less to individual Christians."* He maintains that it was a promise to *"the Apostles collectively,"* "our Lord thus indicating that it was his will that the Church should determine its Faith *collectively,* acting through its constitutional rulers."[8] Dr. Harris stakes everything on this position. The voice of God, he insists, sounds through the Church acting officially as a corporate body. The Catholic Creeds are the official utterances of the Church before it was divided into Roman Catholic and Greek Catholic sections. In the Ecumenical Creeds, therefore, the faith of the Church was determined collectively and

---

[8] *Creeds or No Creeds?*, p. 256.

finally. Then and there the faith of the Church was fixed exactly and unchangeably. And ever thereafter only the Church, "acting through its constitutional rulers," has any right to interpret the Christian Creed. (Note especially that phrase, "constitutional rulers"—as if the Church of Christ could have "rulers," men who lord it over their brethren's faith and practice.) Dr. Harris makes his position perfectly plain. He writes: *"To allow individuals to determine or interpret the Christian Creed spells anarchy."*

All this cuts directly athwart all that Protestantism stands for—all that our Puritan and Huguenot ancestors died for—all that has made possible the freedom of the evangelical churches to-day. The fundamental Protestant principle is that every Christian man has a right to think for himself, and that each humblest Christian may lay claim to Christ's promise of the Spirit to guide him into the truth.

By way of illustrating further the point at issue, it will be recalled that although the Greek Orthodox Church had graciously sent representatives to the Lausanne Conference on Faith and Order, yet when the crucial test came they found it necessary to make their position perfectly plain. Archbishop Germanos, therefore, read a statement signed by the Orthodox delegates, which they had asked him to present to the Conference. In this paper they declared:

"The Orthodox Church adheres fixedly to the principle that the limits of individual liberty of belief are determined by the definitions made by the whole

Church, which definitions we maintain to be obliga-
tory on each individual.

"Therefore, the mind of the Orthodox Church is
that reunion can take place only on the basis of the
common faith and confession of the ancient, undivided
Church of the seven Ecumenical Councils of the first
eight centuries.

"We cannot entertain the idea of a reunion which
is confined to a few verbal statements; for according
to the Orthodox Church, where the totality of the
faith is absent there can be no *communio in sacris.*"

And it is too recent to be forgotten that in Febru-
ary, 1928, Pope Pius XI issued his encyclical, "On
the Promotion of True Religious Unity," a communi-
cation addressed to all Christians in the world not
Roman Catholic. From this I quote briefly:

"The Church was established by Divine Providence
in the world to the end that truths revealed might be
conserved always unchanged, and easily and with
security brought before the notice of men.

"In this Church no one is to be found, as no one
can persevere, who does not recognize and accept
with obedience the supreme authority of Peter and
his legitimate successors.

"Let them" (all the sons who have abandoned the
paternal house) "return to the Common Father,
who, forgetting the injuries they have heaped
upon the Apostolic See, will receive them with all
affection of heart. For if, as they say, they desire to
be united with us and ours, why do they not hasten
to return to the Church, 'Mother and Teacher of
all the followers of Christ.'"

How insistent is this claim to authority to be enforced from without! And how persistent is the
desire, deep-seated in the human mind, to find some
outside prop to lean on in matters of belief and practice! "Now faith is assurance of things hoped for, a
conviction of things not seen." And not having had
"witness borne to them" as did the heroes of the faith
of old and as do the best of Christians to-day, there
are still many good people to be found even in our
Protestant churches who "worship majorities for
want of a reason for their belief" and who look for
some sort of outward authority to determine for them
just what is the faith that has been "delivered unto the
saints."

But our position is that it matters little what your
outward authority is and where it is to be found.
The thing that matters is that you find it necessary to
depend on another and to bow down before the
authorities. "What have I gained," asks Emerson,
"What have I gained that I no longer immolate a bull
to Jove or Neptune, or a mouse to Hecate, or that I
do not tremble before the Eumenides, or the Catholic
Purgatory, or the Calvinistic Judgment Day—if I
quake at opinion? If I quake, what matters it at what
I quake?" And just so we ask, What have I gained
from a spiritual standpoint that I do not bow to the
authority of the Pope, or acknowledge the final
authority in religion and theology of ancient creeds
and councils? If I accept as final any authority that

can be imposed upon me from without, what matters it what authority I accept?

Therefore, as against a creed to be signed, we affirm the value of an inward experience and the necessity of a Christlike life; as against a doctrine of human nature in such wreck and ruin that a revelation from God could come only from without as the Koran was supposed to have been given to the Moham-medans, we affirm that man is essentially akin to God and that within there shines an inner light and there may be heard echoes of the divine voice; as against the religion of the letter, we affirm the religion of the spirit; as against the religion that leans on outward authorities, we affirm the religion of authority—the sole authority of God's voice sounding in the hearts of men.

It will immediately be asked: Is this not a most dangerous position to take? Is not freedom fraught with perils? We answer, Yes, there is danger in this position. But life invests itself with danger. God in his wisdom willed to create free men and not mere things. With freedom comes danger, but also possibility of moral character, possibility of communion with God, the privilege of becoming the children of God, the privilege of knowing the truth and being established in freedom by the truth.

And it needs to be added that there are various ways in which liberty is saved from mere license. There are various methods by which the experience of the single individual is confirmed, or corrected, or held in proper balance. Let some of these be mentioned briefly just now.

Religious experience means much more than "moments of personal awareness of God." One is face to face with God when one feels the compelling power of the True, the Beautiful, and the Good—realities that can be alive only in God and in men made in the image of God. One is face to face with God when conscience cries out in pain over sins committed. And one is face to face with God when one tries to pray and finds somehow a wall shut down between him and the All-Holy because of his having lived down below his best. By religious experience, therefore, we mean much more than our psychologists seem to think we mean when they send out their psychological *questionnaires* and write books on "varieties of religious experience."

Furthermore, our definitely Christian experience is born in society and many things have gone to make that society what it is. We were not set adrift on the sea of life without impulse in any direction and without guide from any source. There are perils enough in traditionalism, but it will be seen that there is much that is of permanent value in traditions—traditions of the family, of the community, and of the Christian Church. And the Bible is the classic book of religious experience. Here is found not the experience of prophets and saints alone, but the experience of all sorts and conditions of men—men of like passions with ourselves. Here, in the Bible, we have a spiritual guide. And into this world of confused ideals and conflicting types of experience came the Son of Man. His soul speaks directly to our deepest selves. He is the very Word of God. He stands as the moral absolute. What he said about God is true. For he spoke with authority. And from the cross where he died there has come the ultimate word touching the dark mystery of human pain, the revelation of the suffering that God endures for the salvation of men—a sacrifice that is reconciling. Down in the heart of our experience "He is our peace." And besides all this, the Church has lived through the centuries, and no matter how dark the period, there have never been wanting Christians who testified victoriously to the inner confirmation of the facts and principles of our religion. In the Christian fellowship, the Church which is "the communion of the saints," continuous witness has been borne to the truth of the gospel. And there are millions living to-day who would die rather than surrender this truth.

Surely the time has come to be done with negative preaching. Hearts are aching for some sure word of prophecy. Too often the people have been like sheep scattered and without a shepherd. Too much have hungry souls broken their teeth on stones offered in the place of bread. Too frequently the blind have led the blind and both have fallen into the ditch. It is now high time that in all pulpits the prophetic voice should speak in tones of authority. The sort of authority the people are waiting for is the authority that comes from God and passes directly to the souls of men. For spiritual authority is always self-authenticating.

> "The word unto the prophet spoken
> Was writ on tables yet unbroken;
> The word by seers and sibyls told,
> In groves of oak, or fanes of gold,
> Still floats upon the morning wind,
> Still whispers to the willing mind.
> One accent of the Holy Ghost
> The heedless world hath never lost."

II

PERILS OF TRADITIONALISM AND VALUES IN TRADITION

"And ye have made void the word of God because of your tradition."—Matthew 15: 6.

II

PERILS OF TRADITIONALISM AND VALUES IN TRADITION

I PURPOSE in the present lecture calling attention to certain perils that lie in traditionalism. This, I trust, will contribute toward a better understanding of what I have in mind in the discussion which is to follow, dealing more directly with the question of authority as it refers to the preacher and his message.

We must, of course, distinguish between *traditionalism* and *traditions*. Traditionalism is an attitude of mind and a habit of life. Our traditions embody many of the most precious possessions of the race, such as our family traditions, our national traditions, and the traditions of faith and heroism that the Church will never willingly let die. And I do confess to some hesitancy in entering upon the discussion of this theme lest my purpose be misapprehended and I be looked upon as an iconoclast ready to lay ruthless hands on the treasured possessions of the race. I say at once, therefore, that there are large values in our traditions; but they must all stand the searchlight of history, they must submit to the test of experience, and they must be tried in the crucible of life. I am not to be understood, then, as meaning that there is nothing but peril in the preservation of traditions. On the contrary I maintain that in them lie racial gains that should by all means be saved to society.

In life and thought there must be not only change and progressive development, there must also be conservation of gains and protection against forces of disintegration. In the physical world there are always two forces at work pulling against each other, the centripetal and the centrifugal, the pull toward the center and the tendency to fly off into space. And the same thing we find in our various ecclesiastical organizations and our different theological systems. Too much pull toward the center gives us traditionalism with its attendant reactionaries, while too great a tendency to fly off at a tangent gives us radicalism and revolutionists. It will be seen as we proceed that I am not speaking in negative terms; I mean to speak in a very positive and affirmative way, and before I have concluded all this will be properly emphasized.

I wish just here to put behind my presentation the supporting words of the Master himself. In the Gospel according to Matthew and in the twenty-third chapter, we read as follows: "For ye build the sepulchres of the prophets, and garnish the tombs of the righteous, and say, If we had been in the days of our fathers, we should not have been partakers with them in the blood of the prophets. Therefore, ye witness to yourselves that ye are sons of them that slew the prophets."

These are very arresting words. What can they mean? How can it be that men will praise the ancient prophets and erect monuments in their honor, flattering themselves that they are congenial spirits bent upon following in their steps, while all the time they are wholly unlike the prophets and are in truth the lineal descendants and legitimate representatives of whose who killed the prophets? In answer I quote a notable paragraph from that Christian classic, *Ecce Homo*:

"The glory of the original man is this, that he does not take his virtues and his views of things at second hand, but draws fresh wisdom from nature and from the inspiration within him. To the majority in every age, that is, the superficial and the feeble, such originality is alarming, perplexing, fatiguing. They unite to crush the innovator. But it may be that by his own energy and by the assistance of his followers, he proves too strong for them. Gradually, about the close of his career, or it may be after it, they are compelled to withdraw their opposition and to imitate the man whom they have denounced. They are compelled to do that which is most frightful to them, to abandon their routine. Then there comes to them a thought which brings inexpressible relief. Out of the example of the original man they can make a new routine. They may imitate him in everything except his originality, for one routine is as easy to pace as another. What they dread is the necessity of originating, the fatigue of being really alive. The original man broke the chains by which men were bound; he threw open to them the doors leading into the boundless freedom of nature and truth. But in the next generation *he* is idolized, and nature and truth as much forgotten as ever. If he could return to the earth, he would find that the crowbars and files with which he made his way out of the prison-house have been forged into the bolts and chains of a new prison called by his own name."

Here lies a danger, the ever-recurrent danger of the dead hand, the traditionalism that worships the past because it is the past and appeals to the God of the dead as against the God of the living.

I

We do this when we rest satisfied in confessing the creeds of our fathers while we ourselves have no living experience of the realities these creeds were originally written to set forth and defend.

Let no man underestimate the importance of the great creeds of Christendom. They are not without their significance. They played an important part in the history of Christianity and they may still be made to serve a place of usefulness in the Church of to-day. The Apostles' Creed, the Nicene Creed, the Lutheran and Reformed Confessions, the Edwardine and Elizabethan Articles—these are most important historic documents, and the history of Christian thought cannot be understood without them. A creed is a milepost; it shows how far the Church had come. A creed is a boundary line; it indicates how large an area of well-defined truth the Church believed it had been able to conquer. A system of thought always lives by the *truth* that is in it, not by the *error* it contains. It lives as it makes vital contact with experience. For example, the Apostles' Creed is both factual and symbolic and therefore remains the one creed in which all Christendom can unite; the Nicene Creed at its heart embodies the hard-earned victory of the Church over Arianism, an alien element which would have disintegrated Christianity if allowed to win the battle; the Thirty-nine Articles of the Church of England are Protestant through and through and of abiding interest and significance to all who trace their spiritual ancestry through English origins. Furthermore, as Martensen has said, "A mind starved by doubt has never been able to produce a dogmatic system." But it needs always be kept in mind that the great truths of religion are not primarily intellectual, that Christianity did not originate in logical propositions, and that it cannot be kept alive by insistence on rigid acceptance of ancient creedal statements. Let it be remembered, then, that the vital truths of Christianity are all truths of experience.

What Christian men had experienced they sought to put into appropriate words, so as to lead others to see the truth as they had seen it, and to experience what had satisfied their souls and transformed their lives. For instance, the very first creed of the Church —"Jesus is Lord"—was to begin with a truth of experience, not something set forth in theological propositions that could be argued into a man's mind. Rather, "No man can say that Jesus is Lord but by the Holy Spirit." Faith in the Holy Trinity—Father, Son, and Holy Spirit—was first given in experience. Afterward effort was made to give intelligent and intelligible expression to this fruitful truth revealed first in the hearts of believers in Jesus. The early Christians were not first theologians and afterward Christians; they were first Christians and later some of them became theologians. And it should not be overlooked that men are never to be called upon first of all to be orthodox and then afterward to become sincere disciples of Jesus. One's moral and spiritual attitudes are of primary importance. The perpetual peril of traditionalism is that it will come to value outward conformity to intellectual statements rather than spiritual sincerity; that it will insist on a form of sound words rather than an inner apprehension of spiritual reality.

Creeds, then, do have their value, but the thing that really matters is the experience that gave birth to the creeds. From history take two familiar illustrations:

What made Martin Luther great, overwhelmingly the mightiest man of his age? Everybody knows the answer. It was his experience of God. God had become to him the Living God. He knew for a certainty what it is to have God to be his God—how God grasps a man and holds him; how faith in God takes away fear and makes a man more than conqueror. There is the swing of the battle-ax and the shout of victory in his great hymn:

"A mighty fortress is our God,
A bulwark never-failing:
Our Helper He, amid the flood
Of mortal ills prevailing."

The Reformation in Germany had its spiritual origin in the soul of the great Reformer.

Permit me to remind you that the Evangelical Revival in the Eighteenth Century called men back to reality. The preachers of the Eighteenth Century believed in the God of the past, but they had little vital faith in the God of the present. They believed in a God who had once spoken, but had no faith in a God who is able to speak now in the human heart. John Wesley, the Oxford scholar and clergyman of the the Church of England, was thoroughly sincere and perfectly orthodox. He was representative of the best in his century, but like others he lacked personal experience of God. It was August Spangenberg, head of the little Moravian community in Georgia, who asked Wesley certain disconcerting questions: "Have you the witness within yourself? Does the Spirit of God bear witness with your spirit that you are a child of God?" Wesley was surprised and did not know what to answer. Wesley's professed creed was sound, but he lacked the experience which interprets and vitalizes the creed. Now a stammering and unsure faith can never move the world. No wonder that hitherto the young clergyman's life had been a disappointment and a failure.

The story of Wesley's evangelical conversion has

become one of the classic things in the study of Christian experience: "In the evening I went to the society in Aldersgate Street, where one was reading Luther's preface to the Epistle to the Romans. About a quarter before nine, while he was describing the change which God works in the heart through faith in Christ, I felt my heart strangely warmed, I felt I did trust in Christ, Christ alone for salvation; and an assurance was given me that he had taken away my sins, even mine, and saved me from the law of sin and death." Straightway Wesley began to tell his experience to others.

That was the beginning of the Evangelical Revival. What Wesley had experienced, others experienced also, and soon England was aflame with a revival movement the warmth of which has not yet wholly cooled down. Wesley and those associated with him still used the same form of words that the Church of England had used, but their words went to the hearts of men with a new message—new because coming out of hearts having a new experience. Here was a new sunrise in Christian history. The lost secret of the power of Christianity had been rediscovered. Their religion became a singing religion. It was their experience that had let loose that "nest of singing birds." In various ways they were all saying:

> "What we have felt and seen
>   With confidence we tell,
>   And publish to the sons of men
>   The signs infallible."

This vital experience of what the creeds stand for —of the everlasting reality behind transient forms— this is what our present age is most interested in. And I must say at once what needs to be understood all along, that by "experience" I mean more than mere emotionalism, much more than "feeling" alone. Mysticism stands for the *noetic* element in religion, that is to say, for the fact that actual knowledge of reality is given in religious experience. Besides this, there is another aspect of the matter that tradition-alists are likely to overlook. The universe is not dead, but alive. Its life is in God, and if I may so speak, God is going somewhere. Purpose is written into the very structure of the world. There is one far-off divine event to which the whole creation is moving. We come to know God not as we sit idly by and study the universe objectively. We can truly know only in fellow-ship with God and coöperation with him. It is, there-fore, when we throw ourselves whole-heartedly into the mighty purpose of God that we come to know God. It is perfectly evident, then, why the *will* as well as the intellect and the emotions must be brought into play if God is to become the Great Reality in our experience and life.

Nothing, therefore, can be more futile than reiter-ated insistence on the part of solemn ecclesiastical assemblies that assent must be given to certain ancient creedal statements before there can be opened a path to Christian unity. It will turn out to be a hopeless task to endeavor to reverse the clock of human history and make it run backward. And besides this, too often creeds have created divisions. Creeds do not bring about unity; the one way to Christian unity is the way of Christian experience. When the Spirit gives us utterance we all speak with united voice. For Pentecostal tongues are always heard as one language.

II

Another peril of traditionalism is that we should remain satisfied to proclaim loyalty to customs and institutions handed down from the past, while we ourselves have no originality nor power of adaptation for the needs of the present.

Now only fools despise the past. If we are to meet the needs of to-day and make wise provision for to-morrow we must know and appreciate what was done yesterday. Certain forces have entered into the making of us, certain principles have become the very life-blood of our people. We cannot break with the past if we would. Wisdom was not born with us. Only as we gather wisdom from the past shall we be able to serve our day and generation according to the will of God. And we modern evangelicals ought to know our own history. Just at the present time I think nothing would be more refreshing and rejuvenating than for the people who have the Protestant inheritance to take up the study of the Reformation in Germany or read once more the marvelous story of the Evangelical Revival in Great Britain and America.

We should then clearly see how our creeds and institutions sprang out of the great experiences of men who had come into communion with God, and how they are rooted in our spiritual past. The interesting question would then arise: How true to the spirit and genius of those early and creative days has been our subsequent development? And we should come face to face with this other question: How far have we departed from that spiritual interpretation of Christianity which was once our power and glory?

But what I have chiefly in mind just now is the fact that antiquity alone is not enough to make a custom binding and of lasting value. Professor Montague, in his interesting study of *The Ways of Knowing,* points out clearly the fallacy of holding that the age of an authority is a mark of its reliability. The familiar saying has it, "As age is wiser than youth, we should revere the opinions of our ancestors." But the opinions and institutions handed down from the fathers were opinions and institutions of their youth and from a time when the race was much younger and more immature than it is now. Their opinions, in many instances, are the expression of the experience and childhood of the race and not its maturity. We ourselves are much older than our ancestors, and are riper in experience than they. It is a hurtful error, therefore, to give to ancient customs and venerable institutions the same respect and reverence that we very properly render to mature and wise men.

An institution handed down from the fathers is

good just as long as it serves a good purpose. A custom is good just as long as it gives opportunity for the free expression of the spiritual life of a people. It has been said that "an institution is the lengthened shadow of a man." It may be something else and worse; it may be a dead hand reaching down from the past and strangling the present. We may indeed build the sepulchres of the prophets and garnish the tombs of the righteous, thinking that we have the spirit of the fathers, when, as a matter of fact, we are the direct descendants of the men who slew them. And, by urgent insistence upon the continuance of certain institutions and customs, we may be curbing the very spirit which formerly found expression in those institutions. Every changeless thing is lifeless; every living thing is changing. Life is a continuous progressive change.

"The old order changeth, yielding place to new,
And God fulfils himself in many ways,
Lest one good custom should corrupt the world."

But let it never be overlooked that prophets do not always start out with the expressed purpose of changing things. Often they are very reluctant of change in customs that have grown hoary with years, and not every man is a prophet who proclaims himself such. Oftener such a man is a false prophet. The true prophet is always modest. He cries, "Ah, Lord God! behold, I cannot speak: for I am a child." He waits and wonders why other men older and better qualified do not speak out in the name of God. He questions for a time whether the voice he hears is after all the voice of God. Then the word within him becomes like fire in his bosom and he can remain silent no longer. He departs from custom only when custom stands in the way of doing what God would have done. He seeks to fill old institutions with new life and establishes new institutions only as new life requires a new way in which to express and perpetuate itself. He seeks to fulfill rather than to destroy.

What I am seeking to emphasize is the fact that serviceable institutions grow out of vital needs and that they are serviceable only so long as they minister to the real values of human society. What I am pleading for is a return of the spiritual experience out of which all worth-while Christian institutions and customs spring. Christianity is a religion growing out of experience; Christian theology is the theology of experience; Christian institutions are institutions shaped by Christian experience to meet the need of the age to which they came. Our fathers and founders, in the first Christian centuries, in the heroic days of the Reformation on the continent of Europe and in England and Scotland, and here in our own land— our fathers, I say, were mighty men of God—men of vision, men of daring, men of action. They were all this because first of all they were men of God and God's free men. John Knox, John Wesley, Jonathan Edwards, Francis Asbury, Phillips Brooks, and others that followed in their train, these saw the sin and sorrow and ignorance of their day; these had prophetic insight to meet living issues as they emerged; these had their faces turned to the future, not to the past; and all these believed in a God who is not far from every one of us—that the God of Abraham, the God and Father of our Lord Jesus Christ, the God of our fathers, is also *our God to-day*, not only the God of the dead, but the God of the living as well.

It is well enough to ask, What is the precedent in such and such a case? It is also the part of wisdom to inquire, What is the usage and what has been the ancient custom? But we have returned to Pharisaical traditionalism when we profess loyalty to ancient institutions as such and are not alive to the needs of the present hour. If our fathers had done no more than this progress would have died at its birth, and we should now be held fast in the icy grip of a dead past.

This is the message that sounds in the Ninety-fifth Psalm. The Psalmist celebrates the glory of God in nature and in the past history of the chosen people, but he breaks forth with the exhortation:

> "To-day, oh that ye would hear his voice!
> Harden not your hearts."

He would have us hear the voice of God in the stirring life of to-day. In the ongoings of the present age God's voice speaks to men. The best and truest Christian, then, is not the one who seeks to do precisely what the fathers did, but the one who meets living issues as the fathers met them, believing in the God of to-day as well as in the God of yesterday.

The traditionalist, on the other hand, if I may borrow a figure, wishing to assure himself of God's interest in human affairs, goes to the stern of humanity's ship and watches the wake far in the rear; but he never stands on the ship's bridge, and feels it sway and turn at the touch of a present Captain in control. The Living God is now in the world. We see him best when we most closely follow his progressively unfolding purpose for men.

III

The traditionalism against which we need to be on our guard is the traditionalism that professes reverence for dead heroes while having none of the spirit of heroism which it claims to hold in high regard.

Reverence for dead heroes is not enough. The age needs living heroes. How great is our condemnation if having a mighty past we ourselves are faint-hearted and afraid in the presence of to-day's demands. For we are living in the midst of stirring days, which call for the best that men can give and do.

And yet, how persistent is that type of mind that lives almost wholly in the past, whose most insistent article of faith is that God was certainly with the ancients! To illustrate: A minister charged with administrative responsibilities was, during a certain gathering of ministers and laymen, telling of new life that had come to an old and long decadent congregation—the ancient and out-of-the-way location had been abandoned, a beautiful church building had been secured on a prominent street, a new educational building was being planned, all church activities had taken on new life—when another minister, who knew something of the situation, walked quietly across the room and inquired, "What became of that old graveyard?" The question was entirely proper. If we are not interested in the graves of our dead we are not worthy of the spiritual inheritance handed down from our fathers. If we do not value our own history we are not qualified to make history for our children. But the question, *"What became of that old graveyard?"* stuck me with considerable force. I had not been thinking about the graveyard. I was at that time thinking about the living and about their children. I was thinking, not of a church standing where monuments had been built to the prophets and where devoted hearts laid flowers on the graves of the righteous, but of a church standing in the midst of the life and activities of a modern city, speaking of Christ to men who had sinned and lost their way, giving inspiration and guidance to the rising generation, and helping to shape in harmony with the principles of the Kingdom of God the institutions of modern society.

And what kind of heroism is it that we need to-day? I answer briefly: The same sort of heroism the Church has always needed: heroism to speak out the thing that is in us regardless of personal consequences;

heroism to live the life which before God we know we ought to live, following not the customs of the day but obeying the voice of God that sounds in the soul; heroism to do the thing we know ought to be done for God and for his Church, whatever that thing may be.

But no man ever made a hero out of himself just by saying that he was going to be one and starting out to do something unusual. Such a man always makes a ridiculous spectacle out of himself like Don Quixote. Heroism is never a manufactured article. It is a living, breathing thing, born out of a great experience. Christian heroism is never born of negations; it is born of affirmations. It never comes from love of the footlights; it abhors the spectacular. It is never self-seeking; it embodies the principle of the cross. It is only when men see deeply into human need and themselves have entered into an experience that satisfies their own needs—it is only then that they are ready to rise to the sublime heights of heroism.

The kind of men described by the Master in the words that suggested the theme of this lecture, men who believe in the voice of God sounding in the past but not in the present, men who believe in institutions and customs fixed and finished by divine authority, men who glory in the vision and daring of the founders of the Church, but call in question the wisdom and sanity of the forward-looking movements of the present time—such men stand squarely across the path of human progress. For, as a matter of fact, the standpatter is the true revolutionary.

I quote from a letter written by Thomas Arnold. Said he: "There is nothing so revolutionary, because there is nothing so unnatural and so convulsive to society, as the strain to keep things fixed, when all the world is by the very law of its creation in eternal progress: and the causes of all the evils in the world may be traced to the natural but deadly error of human indolence and corruption, that our business is to preserve and not to improve. It is the ruin of us all alike, individuals, schools, and nations."[1]

In human history evolution is always better than revolution. Progress is naturally slow and orderly: "first the blade, then the ear, after that the full corn in the ear." Most unfortunately there are many men, sincere and able men some of them are, who view all change with deep alarm. They, therefore, expend their great strength in constant strain to keep things fixed. They are able to do this for a time, it may be a long time. But after a while the push of progress becomes greater than their strength—and suddenly a revolution takes place. The force of an onward-moving stream would naturally carry the logs floating on down to the mill. It is when the logs encounter an eddy or strike a swirl in the current that their onward progress is stayed and they get in a jam; and then it may require dynamite. But it was not the onward-flowing stream that caused the jam; it was

---

[1] Quoted in Batten's *The Social Task of Christianity*, p. 175.

the eddy or the back-wash of the water that did it.
Now a revolution does good; but it is always un-
fortunate, for it does much harm also. It destroys
treasures of faith and life that should continue to
live. But it should be remembered that it is the standpatter who is responsible for revolution. For "the
greatest enemy of progress is not bad men, but good
men who have ceased to grow." And the ultimate
responsibility for the harm done rests always with
the reactionaries.

IV

We are not overlooking the important fact that
there are values in tradition which the race will not
readily consent to lose and without which we shall be
poor indeed.

We shall make no real progress by jauntily plung-
ing into the untried future. The air of too many people
nowadays seems to be, "We don't know where we are
going but we are on the way." Or if not that gay
spirit, then the sad tone of agnosticism:

"Where lies the land to which the ship would go?
Far, far ahead, is all her seamen know.
And where the land she travels from? Away,
Far, far behind, is all that they can say."

If we do not know the land we are sailing from, we
are not likely to know our port of destination. If we
have cared little for the hoarded riches of the past,
we are not likely to care much about any treasure

hidden off somewhere, we do not know where, down below the horizon. The pragmatic method will never bring us to the heart of reality. And the trouble with too many preachers and theologians to-day is that they are mere pragmatists. They do not ask, Is this real? but, Will it work? They are at about the same scientific stage as were the medical doctors of a hundred years ago, their remedies are mostly empirical. They are not sure that they know anything, except they are sure that the past is to be disregarded.

Montague calls attention to the folly of over-emphasis on pragmatism in the tendency to carry to an extreme the elective system in education. I quote, "To leave a child free to study any subject or none is simply to deprive him of his social inheritance. He cannot choose intelligently until he knows what there is to choose *from*. If we wished to make a civilized man out of a savage, we should not take him direct from his forest and put him naked in a department store, bidding him choose whatever clothing caught his fancy. The child is intellectually and culturally naked, and the only life he knows independent of our teaching is the forest life of his instincts. Why should we expect him in the name of 'individuality' and 'self-realization' to repeat all that the race has learned by generations of trial and error? To abstain from all compulsion and all prescription in the teaching of children is, we repeat, merely to rob them of their rightful social heritage."[2]

2*The Ways of Knowing*, p. 142.

Now if this be true in the field of education, it is also certainly true in the sphere of religion. And as a matter of racial experience, the religion of external authority did serve a useful purpose in the education of the race in its childhood. The religion of the Old Testament with its commandments and ordinances was necessary and valuable in its time and place. Not until the time was fulfilled and the race had matured could the religion of the New Testament claim the right to displace the lower order of faith. And during the long period when barbarous races had overrun the Roman Empire and a strong hand was needed to hold them in order, and a rigid discipline required to tame their wild passions, the religion of external compulsion was useful as a schoolmaster to lead them on to higher things.

But beware of the application of this principle; else we shall doom ourselves to perpetual childhood! Only in the exercise of liberty can the highest powers of the soul flourish and grow.

And exactly so with our rightful religious inheritance. For just as riches in civilization, in literature, in art, in music, and in science have come down from the past, so also with religion. It is true that men have been more conservative in religion than in any other department of life, but this is because religion means more to us than science, music, art, letters, or anything else whatsoever. It is our most prized possession. It is our holy thing. It treasures up those interests which have abiding value. It is conservative because it conserves. There are dangers in traditionalism, but there are spiritual values in traditions. If we should beware of the pull toward the center that makes us traditionalists glorying in the past because it is past, we need also to look out for the impulse to fly off at a tangent as seen in the radical and the iconoclast.

And it must be admitted that with numbers of men who call themselves progressive thinkers the love of novelty is greater than the love of truth. The one important question with them seems to be, *Is it new?* They are like a graduate student in some university, perplexed to find a subject for a thesis. He must look through the entire literature to see that nobody ever did it before; then he is ready to proceed. And when we have read what he has to say we feel like saying, "Your thesis is approved. We accept what you have to say as an original piece of work done in scholarly fashion. Now try again sometime with equal diligence to see if you cannot find out what the actual facts are and what the real truth about the matter is." Lovers of novelty among the liberalists remind one of the men of like mind whom Paul in his day encountered in Athens: "They spend their time in nothing else, but either to tell or hear of some new thing." Glibly proclaiming "new truth," they would be willing any time to sacrifice old gold for common tinsel, provided only that the tinsel bore the marks of recent manufacture.

I was recently discussing these matters with one

of the scholarly and progressive ministers of the
Church. I desire to set down here some of the things
he was then saying to me. They are worthy of most
serious consideration.

At the present time, as he suggested, there is an
essential agnosticism seeking shelter in the house of
liberalism. Apostolic Christianity, the Protestant
Reformation, and the Evangelical Revival were all
liberal movements. The freedom they desired was
to clear away the restrictions of externalism for a
better growth of the spirit as the motivating power
of the new religious order. In the religious movements just mentioned three things at least were held
in common: First, the sinfulness of man and of
society was clearly and fully recognized; secondly,
the power of the gospel of Christ to save individuals
and the world was asserted with all confidence;
thirdly, the Christian duty of proclaiming this salvation at all costs was accepted by all these liberal
believers. It appears now, however, that one wing
of the liberal movement in our churches has drifted
far from the liberalism of the New Testament, the
Protestant Reformation, and the Evangelical Revival. These new liberals seem to have a decided
leaning in the direction of agnosticism. From the
souls of some of these men doubt has taken away
nearly all positive conviction as to the validity of the
historic faith. Hence there is no enthusiasm for the
conversion of the world, either as to the potency
of the gospel in this respect, or indeed as to the need

of conversion itself. They spurn the past; but they have discovered no new method of salvation that the world would think of trusting. By mere inertia such persons are in the Church seeking a negative liberalism as a means of security against responsibility and sacrifice.

Moreover, it should be noted that Paul, Luther, and Wesley were all by native instinct and religious conviction conservative. They did not break with the ecclesiasticisms of their day till forced to do so, nor until they broke their own hearts in disappointed loyalty.

Our most significant religious values are to be found in *history* and in *experience*. History brings over the inheritance of the past; experience lives in touch with the present. Also experience puts to the test the value of history. It is never safe, it is always dangerous, to depart from tradition except in the light and under the guiding influence of experience. And by experience in this connection is meant not the isolated experience of individuals only. Adequate personal experience must be rooted in racial experience. Satisfactory Christian experience must grow out of and be in harmony with the vital faith of the Christian Church. Not the single individual is the final authority, but the experience of the individual coming to birth in the Christian community, confirmed by the Christian brotherhood, and corroborated by the experience of the past. The living present must grow out of the fruitful past.

It is not to be wondered at that Jesus startled the traditionalists of his day. They could not fail to see that his teachings were creating a stir and were likely to upset their entire system of legalism and ritualism. But Jesus was not a destroyer. Everything good in the old he loved. One jot or one tittle would in no wise pass away till it had served its rightful purpose, and the vital principle in it had been fulfilled. Said he: "Think not that I came to destroy the law or the prophets: I came not to destroy, but to fulfill." And even so, at the present time, timid and fearful souls are often startled by the ring of reality sounding in modern voices. Such originality is alarming and perplexing. They are afraid that the very foundations will be destroyed. The opportunity of the modern preacher is to be found in following the way of the Master and saying to all who are troubled: *Think not that we have come to destroy: we have not come to destroy, but to fulfill.*

III

AUTHORITY AND THE BIBLE

"Every scripture inspired of God is also profitable for teaching, for reproof, for correction, for instruction which is in righteousness: that the man of God may be complete, furnished completely unto every good work."—II Timothy 3: 16–17.

III

AUTHORITY AND THE BIBLE

THE historical method of studying the Bible has opened a door into the treasure house of Holy Scripture which no man can now shut. The Bible to us is a much more human book, and also much more divine, than it was to our fathers. Unfortunately, the wine of the new knowledge has frequently gone to the head, and some preachers, in a manner wholly academic and unspiritual, have raised doubts in the mind and brought distress to the heart where positive and affirmative presentation would have brought relief and comfort and reassurance. The Bible of the modern preacher is not a smaller Book than was the Bible of our fathers, but larger and more authoritative—"inspired of God and profitable for teaching, for reproof, for correction, for instruction which is in righteousness: that the man of God may be complete, furnished completely unto every good work."

You will permit a preacher whose life has been spent almost entirely in the pastorate and pulpit to give personal testimony. A generation ago George Adam Smith's *Isaiah* had just been published. That was at the beginning of my ministry. I had been try-

ing to find out something about the Old Testament.
Nothing that I had read satisfied me. My commentaries and Biblical histories helped very little. It
was then that Smith's great exposition came from the
press. I read the two volumes with wonder and
delight. The book of *Isaiah* was no longer made up
of detached utterances hanging up in the air. Here
was a flesh-and-blood man with a living message to
the age in which he lived. Often as I read Smith's
pages I was not able to keep my seat; I would get up
and walk the floor. I read Isaiah at family worship;
I preached on Isaiah Sunday after Sunday. I knew
that in discovering Isaiah I had discovered the Old
Testament. One day when I had come home from
my study and dinner was about to be served, I was
asked to get a bucket of water. I went to the cistern
thinking about Isaiah—only Isaiah—and down into
the cistern I let bucket, rope and all! I tell this story
because, as a matter of fact, I had let my bucket down
not into a cistern, but into a well of living water, and
out of that well I have been drawing water ever
since. From the time George Adam Smith introduced
me to Isaiah, the entire Old Testament began to take
its proper place in my spiritual life, and in the entire
Bible I hear sounding the Word of God. By introduc-
ing me to the historical method, Smith had introduced me to the whole Bible.

What is to be said in the present lecture is of a
positive and affirmative character. But it seems neces-

sary at once to make a few preparatory remarks of a somewhat negative nature.

(1) Bacon, in one of his essays, speaks of the Bible as having been written by "the pencil of the Holy Ghost." Now nothing has been more mischievous in the history of Christian thought than the "verbal dictation theory" of the inspiration of the Bible. This theory, of course, has no basis in the Bible itself, and upon even the most hurried examination of the pages of the Bible it is seen to be contrary to the facts in the case. But still the opinion persists that the very words of the Bible were dictated by the Holy Spirit and that they are authoritative and infallible in all matters, whether of history, or of science, or of faith. Well, it has not pleased God to give us that kind of Bible. And for this we are devoutly thankful.

(2) And there is the companion view, that the Bible is all on one level and that any one part of it is of equal value and authority with any other part. But an examination of any devout Christian's Bible would disprove that theory at once. There are parts of the Bible where the saints live; there are other parts where they occasionally make visits; there are other parts where they never go at all—or if they do, it is in blind devotion and without spiritual profit. And certain men of spiritual intuition saw this long before the method of historical approach had brought moral relief. Luther, by way of illustration, felt free to say that the Epistle of James was "an epistle of

straw." In that Luther was wrong. And John Wesley, in the Psalter which he prepared for the American Methodists, left out the imprecatory Psalms entirely, and in doing so added this comment: "Many psalms are left out, and many parts of others, as highly improper for the mouths of a Christian congregation." In that Wesley was exactly right.

(3) Let it be clearly understood, then, that the revelation conveyed through the Bible comes through a long historical process and was necessarily gradual and progressive.

For education is always a slow process, both because we must wait for the child to grow and because knowledge is never a ready-made article that can be transferred bodily into the human mind. And just so with the spiritual education of the race, slowly and painfully does the race rise. Slowly and painfully does the race learn its moral and spiritual lessons, going forward a little and then slipping back and then starting over again. The Epistle to the Hebrews sees this plainly: "God having of old time spoken unto the fathers in divers portions and in divers manners, hath at the end of these days spoken unto us in his Son." In many parts and in many ways God spoke. The revelation was piecemeal, coming as it did through many spokesmen and through different ages and to people variously circumstanced, and coming in different modes—through history, prophecy, the words of the Wise Men, and the psalms of many singers.

Always the significance and value of a process must be judged not from its lowly beginnings but from what it produces in the final outcome. We judge the possibilities of an acorn from an oak; we judge the value of a bud from the flower; we judge the significance of the babe in its mother's arms from the value of the strong man to society. And we judge the Bible properly when in it we hear sounding, at the completion of a long process, the full tones of the divine voice. Which is to say, the early beginnings of revelation in the Old Testament must be read in the light of the messages of the great prophets; the Old Testament in its entirety must be read in the light of the New Testament; and the entire Bible must be read in the light of Jesus.

What has just been said may seem to be entirely superfluous, but it is not, for among the majority of church members unenlightened notions still continue to damage their faith. And quite frequently we are surprised at criticisms directed at Christianity from college professors and university men. When we read what they sometimes say we wonder what these men have been doing that so successfully they have kept their shutters closed to the morning light so persistently beating against their windows. And we wonder, too, what we preachers have been doing that we have failed to bring the light to intelligent and open-minded men.

Now when we take up the study of the Bible from the historical method of approach, speaking broadly

we see in the Holy Scripture three things: First, we
have here the history of the Hebrews from the call of
Abraham to the coming˙of Jesus and the beginnings
of the Christian Church; secondly, we have the
literature of a highly gifted people, preserving the
best of the ethical and spiritual teachings of the
prophets and giving the wonderful words which fell
from the lips of the supreme Master; and thirdly, we
have an account of the religious experience of many
men, in different lands, down to the time of the New
Testament when Jesus spoke of his fellowship with
the Father and the apostles told of the meaning to
them in experience of Jesus himself.

Let us think of these three aspects of the Bible
separately and in the order given.

I

The Bible presents an outline of the history of the
Hebrew people leading on up to the story of Christ
and the beginnings of the Christian Church.

Now history as such is not self-authenticating.
This is to say history is not a matter of faith, but
rather a subject for belief. Any record purporting to
recite history must stand or fall with the evidence
brought forward in its support. Now belief is simply
the acceptance of evidence. Belief is purely an intellectual matter. There is nothing necessarily moral
in it. A man cannot will to believe that Moses wrote
the Pentateuch. Nor can he will to believe that Paul
wrote the letter to the Galatians. If the evidence does

not convince him, then he cannot believe it. On the other hand, if the evidence is sufficient, then he has no recourse—he must believe. As we shall see a little later on, there is much in the Bible that can be tested by experience. What produced experience, experience can verify. But such questions as the authorship of a book in the Bible, or the composition of a book, or the date of its writing—these questions cannot be settled by reference to faith. And the same thing is true of facts of history. Whether the things written about Abraham, or Moses, or Elijah are in exact harmony with the facts of history—none of these things falls within the realm of faith; all fall within the realm of intellectual belief. None of these things can be tested in religious experience; all must be submitted to exactly the same tests that we apply when studying the history of Rome or the history of China.

It will appear, however, as we proceed with these lectures that there is a point where facts of history become matters of faith. The history of the Hebrew people and, in a very special way, the history given in the New Testament, at certain well-defined points becomes the history of the deeds of God, rather than the acts of men. The Hebrews did certainly view some of the great events of their history in this light. The call of Abraham, the deliverance of the people from Egyptian bondage, the restoration after the captivity in Babylon—these and many other things they looked upon as acts of God. Of such things as these they wrote:

> "Jehovah doth build up Jerusalem;
> He gathered together the outcasts of Israel.
>
> .   .   .   .   .   .
>
> He hath not dealt so with any nation;
> As for his ordinances, they have not known them.
>   Praise ye Jehovah."

And we who are Christians build our religion on the faith that in Jesus Christ God appears visibly upon the earth, and that the redemptive deeds of Jesus are the acts of God. Furthermore, we are convinced that where the sphere of history is the scene of redemptive deeds the acts of God become self-authenticating. We dare affirm that when God actually appears man is so made that he can see him. But we shall have more to say about this in subsequent lectures.

And let this also be kept clearly in mind: the trustworthiness of the Bible as a vehicle of revelation does not stand or fall with belief in the scientific accuracy of all its narratives. History wherever found is subject to all the canons of historical study. We ask nothing special for the Bible in this respect. We do, however, make bold to ask that the Bible be treated not unfairly, that students bring to it the same openness of mind and intellectual fairness that they would properly bring to the study of the records of any other ancient people.

All that really concerns us is the fundamental trustworthiness of the main outlines of history contained in the Bible. The details do not matter. The only thing that does matter is that we accept the Bible as giving in the Old Testament, in broad outline, the story of preparation for the advent of Christ; and that we see in the New Testament the supreme achievement of God's purpose through the Hebrew people, namely, the fulfillment of their hopes and ideals in the coming of Jesus.

And we do not discount the importance of history. It is not a weakness of the Christian religion, but rather a point of strength, that we see in the Bible a foundation for our faith both in history and in experience. "For," to quote A. S. Peake, "if the proof from experience has its limitations, so also, as every historical critic knows only too well, has the argument from history. Let alone, neither can bear the weight of the Christian case. Locked in an arch, when each supports the other, we can securely trust our faith to them."[1]

II

In the Bible we have the loftiest ethical teaching to be found in all the literature of the world. And this ethical teaching is self-authenticating.

We have already seen that the revelation of God and of His truth, of necessity, came gradually. We

---

[1] *The Bible: Its Origin, Its Significance and Its Abiding Worth,* p. 473.

have suggested that there has come immense moral relief to Christian men in understanding something about the slow and age-long progress of the Hebrews toward an understanding of the highest ethical ideals. To illustrate: Abraham's faith set him apart as the father of the faithful, but much that Abraham does is on the moral level of his time. Samson's bad morals and bad manners are quite offensive, but he has discovered the power of faith. David was in a certain sense a man after God's own heart, but David would not be admitted to membership in any of our churches to-day. The well-instructed Christian of the Twentieth Century finds no difficulty in such matters. He now knows how to read his Bible, namely, as *the record of God's progressive self-revelation in history and in experience, growing from less to more and from more to more still until the supreme hour comes and Christ stands on earth as the Word of God made flesh.*

The long period of preparation in the early history of Israel comes to completion in the Eighth Century with the coming of the great prophets of a pure, ethical monotheism, that is to say Amos and Hosea and those who came after them. In the light of their teaching all lower standards are superseded. And it is affirmed that their lofty moral messages need no higher authority than themselves to enforce them. They shine in their own light.

Amos was a countryman. His home had been in the "wilderness of Tekoa." In the loneliness of his

country life he had meditated on the sins of the
Northern Kingdom. Wealth and luxury had brought
with them all their attendant evils. The rulers aped
the fashions of their neighbors, lolling on soft-cush-
ioned divans, drinking wine and singing foolish songs.
Rich men trampled on the rights of the poor, and
for the debt of "a pair of shoes" sold them into
slavery. Religion seemed to share in the outward
prosperity. Gilgal, Dan, and Beersheba were filled
with crowds of worshippers. Tithes and sacrifices
were offered in lavish abundance. But utterly hollow
and immoral it all was. Then suddenly appeared
Amos with his cry of justice:

"Hear this, ye that trample the needy,
  And oppress the poor of the land,
  Saying, When will the New Moon pass,
  That we may sell our corn.
  And the Sabbath; that we may open
  And sell the refuse of grain,
  Making the ephah small and the shekel great,
  And forging scales of deceit?

. . . . . .

"By the glory of Jacob hath Jehovah sworn
  Your deed I will never forget!
I will turn your feasts into mourning,
  And all your songs into dirges.
I will bring up sackcloth on all your loins,
  And baldness on every head:
And I will make it like mourning for an only son,
  And the end thereof as a bitter day."[2]

---

[2]Gordon's translation in *The Prophets of the Old Testament*.

Amos's message of social righteousness, based upon his knowledge of the righteous character of Israel's God, stands for all time—and especially for the time in which we prosperous Americans now live. It speaks with authority, the authority of ultimate and everlasting truth.

In a very special manner Hosea's message came out of his own sad and broken heart. In his time of bitter sorrow God had come near and revealed himself to him. It is a message of divine love and compassion. He had loved a woman, Gomer by name. But she had not loved him. She had proved false to him and sold herself to other lovers. But Hosea loved her still and brought her back home in spite of all her adultery and shame. With the deep and passionate love of utter purity he had loved her. And now "he boldly transferred his human affections to God. Uplifted by them, he stormed the heavens by his love." In the words of his prophecy we can hear the very heart throbs of the divine compassion:

"How can I give thee up, Ephraim—
    Abandon thee, Israel?
How can I make thee like Admah,
    Treat thee like Zeboim?

"My heart is turned within me,
    My compassions are kindled together;
I cannot work out the heat of my wrath,
    I cannot make havoc of Ephraim.
For I am God, and not man—

The holy one in thy midst;
I come no more to consume [thee]."[3]

The tenderness of Hosea's message finds no equal in Holy Scripture till he came who told of the lost sheep—"and he layeth it on his shoulders, rejoicing"; and told also of the son who had gone into the far country and came back home again—and his father "ran, and fell on his neck and kissed him."

In full accord with Amos and Hosea are the prophecies of Isaiah, who saw the Lord high and lifted up, and interpreted all religion and all human duties in the light of his awful holiness; and the preaching of the heartbroken Jeremiah, who identified himself fully with the suffering of his people and lost his life in their service.

In the century following Amos and Hosea the truth concerning God's requirements and man's obligation finds perfect and final expression in the prophet Micah, where Israel asks what God requires, and God makes answer through the mouth of his servant:

Israel inquires:

"Wherewith shall I come before the Lord,
And bow myself before the high God?
Shall I come before him with burnt offerings,
With calves of a year old?
Will the Lord be pleased with thousands of rams,
Or with ten thousands of rivers of oil?
Shall I give my first born for my transgression,
The fruit of my body for the sin of my soul?"

[3]Gordon's translation in *The Prophets of the Old Testament.*

And God answers:

"He hath shown thee, O man, what is good;
And what doth the Lord require of thee,
But to do justly,
And to love mercy,
And to walk humbly with thy God."[4]

These lofty messages, I say, need no authority beyond themselves. One recalls the well-known saying of Kant's, that there are two things which the oftener he contemplated them the more did they fill him with admiration and wonder, namely, the starry heavens above him and the moral law within him. And when one reads Amos and Hosea and Micah and others of the great prophets the moral law within utters a profound Amen to the moral law as set forth by these messengers of God. By the authority of "the inward Sinai" their teachings are declared to have come from God.

And this process of gradual revelation comes to its supreme completion in Jesus Christ. In very truth does Christ fulfill the prophets. What they saw truly, he reaffirms. What they saw dimly, he saw clearly; what was revealed to them in part, is revealed fully in him. Thus God spoke "in his Son"—not through him as a passive instrument, not in his words alone, but "*in* his Son." And here part the two historic theories of Christianity, "whether the Gospel is law or life, whether the Lord's teaching or his Person is

---

[4]*The Hebrew Prophets,* by F. H. Woods and F. E. Powell, Vol. I, p. 179.

the final truth." We hold that the supreme message of the Bible is in the Person of Christ. In his Son, God hath spoken. Here the heart of God has uttered itself. In him the secret of the universe is told.

Canon Streeter in his book, *Reality,* has a thoughtful chapter on "The Christ." One follows Streeter with increasing interest all the way to his conclusion: *"It is in no impoverished sense that we recite the ancient phrase, Christ is of 'one substance with the Father'; and to describe Him we shall find no words more true than 'Son of God.'"* But Streeter tells us that when finally he read in proof his chapter on "The Christ," there came over him a feeling of acute dissatisfaction. In discussing problems about Christ he had seemed to miss the Christ himself. Then he adds these significant words: "But perhaps that does not really matter. The Gospels are there; from their pages who will may find the Master's personality in all its grace and majesty." And this in truth is quite remarkable. The evangelists were not taught in the schools; they knew nothing of art. But what perfect artists they were! In what sharp contrast they stand with the writers of the Apocryphal gospels, pitifully puerile. And although beginning with such fine studies as we have in *Ecce Homo* and ending with Bruce Barton's *The Man That Nobody Knows,* whom Barton seems to know quite well as a down-to-date American business man, all kinds of *Lives* of Christ have in these latter years been coming constantly from the pen of scholars, Christian, Jew, and others of no faith—not one of these *Lives* is satisfactory; all are disappointing. But this does not really matter, for the four Gospels do not disappoint us. They constantly amaze us. However the story came to be told, here it is. However the picture got itself together, here is the picture of Christ. We read these Gospels and see in them a sort of perpetual incarnation. That great statement at the end of the prologue to the Fourth Gospel sums it up: "No man hath seen God at any time; the only begotten Son, who is in the bosom of the Father, he hath declared him." When we read the gospel story this fact is brought home to our hearts. This also is a statement of fact, not the presentation of a theory.

And let it be observed that nowhere does Jesus in his teaching deal in mere rules of correct behavior. Rather he enunciates fundamental principles in the light of which men must reach their own decisions touching the details of their conduct.

"Moreover, the decisions at which He arrived, in their fundamental principles, hold good against all lapse of time. When moral and religious advance is made it is not true to say that it antiquates the teaching of Jesus; on the contrary, it presents itself as a fresh unfolding of what Jesus meant. The more His Gospel goes out into the wider world, the more clearly does it exhibit its universal character."[5]

Professor George John Romanes was greatly impressed with this consideration at the time he was

---

[5]Dodd, *The Authority of the Bible,* p. 282.

painfully working his way back from atheism to Christian faith. He states it thus:

"One of the strongest pieces of objective evidence in favor of Christianity is not sufficiently enforced by apologists. Indeed, I am not aware that I have ever seen it mentioned. It is the absence from the biography of Christ of any doctrines which the subsequent growth of human knowledge—whether in natural science, ethics, political economy, or elsewhere—has had to discount. This negative argument is really almost as strong as the positive one from what Christ did teach."[6]

But to Jesus himself, let it be emphasized, rather than to anything he said and taught, must we always turn to see the fullest manifestation of the spiritual and the ethical—the perfect revelation of moral love raised to the highest. In him is no imperfection; in him is every holy quality.

"But Thee, but Thee, O sovereign Seer of time,
But Thee, O poet's poet, Wisdom's tongue,
But Thee, O man's best Man, O love's best Love,
O perfect life in perfect labor writ,
O all men's Comrade, Servant, King or Priest—
What *if* or *yet,* what mole, what flaw, what lapse,
What least defect, or shadow of defect,
What rumor, tattled by an enemy,
Or inference loose, what lack of grace
Even in torture's grasp, or sleep's or death's,—
Oh, what amiss may I forgive in Thee,
Jesus, good Paragon, thou Crystal Christ?"

---

[6] *Thoughts on Religion*, p. 167.

Now all this—the growing revelation of the righteous character of God, culminating in the writing of the great prophets; the teachings of Jesus, filling to the full the teachings of the Old Testament; and most of all the life of Christ, carrying it all up to perfection —all this, we have here in the Bible. And it can be found nowhere else in the literature of the world. This does make an imperative appeal to men. Thus does the Word of God find us and find us in the deepest places of our being.

III

We have seen that in the Bible is to be found *history* and the sublimest *ethical teaching*. We now call attention to the fact that the Bible is preëminently a book of personal religious experience.

Indeed, this is the most characteristic and most essential feature of the Bible. And if there had not been deep and satisfying experience of religious reality on the part of the men who wrote the Bible, the history would not have been recorded and the literature of instruction in righteousness would never have been written. It is the experience that makes the recorded history worth while and the ethical teachings profoundly significant.

The men of the Bible are sure that they have met God. Call over certain names and see what the very mention of their names has to suggest: Abraham, the friend of God; Enoch, who walked with God; Moses, who endured as seeing him who is invisible; Samuel, who heard God's voice when only a little child in Eli's house; David, strong to do battle because of his faith in God; Isaiah, who saw the Lord high and lifted up and had the revelation of his holiness; Jeremiah, whose heart was broken with the afflictions of his people and who found solace through fellowship with God; and John the Baptist, who through communion with God in the desert gained the strength of Elijah. I will dare also to mention the name of Jesus, who lived so close to the borders of the other world that once the light of it shot him through and through and his very garments became strangely white. Paul also will I name, to whom was given a vision of the risen Jesus and who tells us that once he was caught up to the third heaven and heard things not lawful to utter.

Also the Bible tells of experience as bringing new power for moral living. All the experiences mentioned above have value for daily life and for heroic endeavor. And it is because of its definitely ethical quality that all religious experience recorded in the New Testament becomes especially significant. The Spirit of God in the New Testament is more than a Spirit giving great physical strength, or a Spirit giving cunning as to a skilled workman, or a Spirit giving wisdom to the wise, or a Spirit giving power and knowledge to do battle against one's enemies. The Spirit of God in the New Testament is the Holy Spirit, *essentially holy* and *creating holiness.*

The Synoptic Gospels would never have been written but for the experience of Christ as the Son of the Living God. And what a book of experience is the Fourth Gospel! Herein lies its priceless value: What Jesus had been to John and what Jesus was to the Church at the end of the First Century, all that is here in this book called John's Gospel, the best-loved book in the New Testament. Furthermore, what Paul and the others do, in the remaining books of the New Testament, is to let all men know what Jesus Christ had come to mean to them in their own personal experience.

The Bible, then, is the classic book of religious experience. It contains the most valuable collection in existence of utterances out of personal experience touching the meaning of religion. It is a collection of testimonials to Christian experience from various men, in different lands, and under various circumstances of life.

Here also in the Bible is an experience of another kind—a deep and satisfying experience of companionship with the Father which brings a new feeling of value to life and a new meaning to human personality. This experience led some of the Old Testament saints to feel sure that God would not let them lie forever in the grave. Thus writes one of the psalmists:

"But God will redeem my soul from the power of
    Sheol;
        He will receive me."

Another goes on with complete faith to say:

"Thou wilt guide me with thy counsel,
    And afterwards receive me to glory.
Whom have I in heaven but thee?
    And there is none upon earth that I desire besides
        thee.
My flesh and my heart faileth:
    But God is the strength of my heart and my
        portion forever."

This faith in immortality seen rarely in some of the Old Testament saints is traceable directly to their experience of fellowship with the Living God.

When we pass to the New Testament this confidence is triumphant. The question will, of course, be raised: Can immortality be a matter of experience? And the answer will at once be given that immortality as *endless life* cannot possibly be an experienced fact. But in the New Testament, and especially the Fourth Gospel, *eternal life* is far more than endless existence. It is quality of life. And whosoever has faith in Christ already has the quality of life that is destined to survive death and outlast time. This kind of life is to Christians of to-day a matter of experience. And here again does the Bible authenticate itself in living experience.

In this particular the truth of the Bible is supremely authoritative. While it is such a record of religious experience as cannot be found anywhere else in the world, the religious experiences described therein are not unlike our own. For we too have experience of religious reality, and when we go to the Bible we see that the men of the Bible had the same needs and the same fulfillment of those needs that we ourselves have had. Here in the Bible are heard the cries of broken and contrite hearts, and we know what those cries mean. Here are sinners who have received power to live a new life of faith, and we too have by faith come into newness of life. Here in the Bible are stories of men who had fellowship with God and to whom the unseen world was the real world. Upon us this visible world presses with insistence every day and the fellowship we have with God is often broken. But when we read what faith meant to the men of the Bible in power to overcome the world and to walk with God, while we stand condemned for our shortcomings, we find victorious hope springing up within us that we also shall attain some day to perfection of faith and steadfastness of life. Sometimes we have had deep and satisfying experiences. But they are transitory: they come and go; and we wonder then whether or not we had them at all. But when we turn to the Bible, here they all are. Here is a great cloud of witnesses to the everlasting reality of our religion. And here the Bible speaks home to our hearts with a message of compelling power.

For these reasons the Bible has been the friend and companion of holy and heroic souls through all the centuries. And for these reasons the Bible is an eternal book.

IV

If now again we ask, Where lies the authority of the Bible? we shall say once more that the authority of the Bible lies within the truth which the Bible itself teaches, validated in the corporate experience of the Church and the experience of all the individuals of the family of God.

There cannot possibly be any authority outside of and beyond the Bible with power to enforce the authority of the Bible. The Bible needs no such authority. For in the realm of the intellectual and spiritual external authority is simply out of place. And religion is such an intimate and personal thing that to talk about enforcing it from without is simply an impertinence.

But as everybody knows, the religion of external authority holds that the authority of the Bible traces back to the authority of the Church and that it was the Church that gave the Bible to the world. I quote from an able advocate of this view:

"By a strange inconsistency, the Modernist, who denies the right of the Church Universal to determine the Christian Creed, does not contest its right to determine the canon of Scripture. The Church, as everyone knows, existed before any New Testament book was written, and possessed a defined Creed before there was a canon of the New Testament at all. Nor is it denied by any, that not the least important of the tests which a book claiming admission into the canon had to pass was the test of orthodoxy."[7]

With Dr. Harris's position we are in complete disagreement. We call attention to the point at issue. The evangelical Christian denies the right of any ecclesiasticism to determine what the canon of Scripture shall be, and also denies the power of the Church to decide what any man shall believe. No General Council determined what books should go into the Bible. And to say that the Church as an ecclesiasticism existed before there was a Bible and had a standard of orthodoxy by which to test all books proposed for admission into the canon, is not to write history but to write fables. For the books that finally went into the canon were only the books that had already been able to win their way to the hearts of Christian people. Various religious writings had been sifted out by the Christian consciousness, and before *that* court had been found to have authority. The final decision of the Church simply registered an accomplished fact. The final authority then as now was in the high council of the Christian soul.

And this position cannot properly be spoken of as "Modernistic." On the contrary, it is in perfect harmony with the claims of the Bible itself, and is the position taken with reference to the authority of

[7] *Creeds or No Creeds?*, pp. 255–256.

the Bible that won its way during the days of the Reformation.

"In describing the authoritative character of Scripture, the Reformers always insisted that its recognition was awakened in believers by that operation which they called the witness of the Holy Spirit (*Testimonium Spiritus Sancti*). Just as God Himself makes us know and feel the sense of pardon in an inward experience by faith which is His own work, so they believed that by an operation of the same spirit, believers were enabled to recognize that God is speaking authoritatively in and through the words of Scripture."[8]

Said Professor Robertson Smith, speaking in perfect harmony with the faith of Protestantism:

"If I am asked why I receive Scripture as the word of God, and as the only perfect rule of faith and life, I answer with all the fathers of the Protestant Church, *Because the Bible is the only record of the redeeming love of God, because in the Bible alone I find God drawing near to men in Christ Jesus, and declaring in Him His will for our salvation. And this record I know to be true by the witness of His Spirit in my heart, whereby I am assured that no other than God Himself is able to speak such words to my soul.*"[9]

God's Word and the human soul need no third party. The divine revelation speaks directly to the heart of man.

---

[8]Lindsay, *The Reformation in Germany,* p. 461.
[9]Quoted in Denney's *Studies in Theology,* pp. 204-205.

". . . the Truth in God's breast
Lies trace for trace upon ours impressed:
Though he is so bright and we are so dim,
We are made in his image to witness him:

"And were no eye in us to tell,
Instructed by no inner sense,
The light of heaven from the dark of hell,
That light would want its evidence."

And a study of the Bible itself will show that it is just here that it bases its authority to speak to men. The Bible makes no other claims, nor does it need any other.

At no time did the Old Testament prophet make any appeal to any historic ecclesiasticism to back him up, nor did he appeal to any venerable creed to give him support. Thus spoke Amos: "Thus saith the Lord," and again, "Thus saith the Lord." And when his words alarmed Amaziah the priest and Jeroboam the king and they commanded him to flee away to his own land, the land of Judah, and there receive support as a professional prophet and prophesy there, Amos made answer: "I was no prophet, neither was I a prophet's son: but I was a herdsman and a dresser of sycamore trees: and the Lord took me from following the flock, and the Lord said unto me, Go, prophesy unto my people Israel. *Now, therefore, hear thou the word of the Lord.*" That, and that alone, was his authority, and still through all the centuries do we hear "the word of the Lord" sounding through his message. In like manner spoke all the prophets, believing that the soul of man will respond when confronted by the word of the Lord, and that the word of the divine message will win its own way.

And in exactly the same way did Paul the apostle speak. See how he puts the matter in his second letter to the Corinthians:

"Therefore seeing we have this ministry, even as we have obtained mercy, we faint not: but we have renounced the hidden things of shame, not walking in craftiness, nor handling the word of God deceitfully, but by the manifestation of the truth, commending ourselves to every man's conscience in the sight of God. And even if our gospel is veiled, it is veiled in them that are perishing; in whom the god of this world hath blinded the minds of the unbelieving, that the light of the gospel of the glory of Christ, who is the image of God, should not dawn upon them. For we preach not ourselves, but Christ Jesus as Lord, and ourselves as your servants for Jesus' sake. Seeing it is God that said, Light shall shine out of darkness, who shined in our hearts, to give the light of the knowledge of the glory of God in the face of Jesus Christ."

Linger for a moment at that phrase, "commending ourselves to every man's conscience in the sight of God"—just throwing out the light into the darkness and letting it shine there, just appealing to the human conscience and resting the appeal there. It was none of the apostle's business to back up his message with authorities; his business was to proclaim his gospel.

His object was not to "form an irrefragable argument, but to produce an irresistible impression."

To conclude, here in the Bible is the recorded history of a people called and chosen, through whom the highest type of religion has come into the world, as Art came through the Greeks and Law through the Romans. Here is the wisdom of wise men sifted through the centuries. Here is the message of the prophet telling of God who is holy, just, and good. Here are messages of social righteousness preserved sacredly by the very people whose sins were therein rebuked. Here are books like Job and Ecclesiastes going down to the bottom of the problem of sorrow and the seeming vanity of all life—and waiting for some sure word of God yet to come. Here are the psalms of the Hebrew singers, breaking with sorrow or welling up out of hearts made glad by a sense of the Divine presence and through the peace of sins forgiven. And here in the Bible is the story of Jesus, the saddest and most tragic, the gladdest and most triumphant story ever told. Here also is the outlook upon a better world, the certain confidence in a better time coming when God shall make all things new. And here, too, is the promise and hope of immortality. To these men of the Bible, imperfectly in the Old Testament and then with overwhelming clarity and power in the New, the meaning and value of human personality became so sure and the joy of fellowship with the living God so intensely real, that at last, in the very face of Death they were able to say, "O death, where is thy victory? O death, where is thy sting? . . . Thanks be to God, who giveth us the victory through our Lord Jesus Christ."

To use the language of Edmond Sherer:

"The Bible will ever be the book of power, the marvelous book, the book above all others. It will ever be the light of the mind, the bread of the soul. Neither the superstition of some nor the irreligious negations of others have been able to do it harm. If there is anything certain in the world, it is that the destinies of the Bible are linked with the destiny of holiness on earth."[10]

[10]Quoted in *Religions of Authority*, p. 249.

IV

THE BASIS OF AUTHORITY IN HISTORY

"For other foundation can no man lay than that which is laid, which is Jesus Christ."—I CORINTHIANS 3: 11.

IV

THE BASIS OF AUTHORITY IN HISTORY

THE religion of the Bible rests upon a twofold basis, a basis in history and a basis in experience. The Christian religion is concerned supremely about Jesus Christ. He is a fact of history. He is also a fact of experience. Here, in him, we find the ultimate basis of authority for our faith.

I recognize at once that this ties up Christianity with human history. Not only do I recognize this: I rejoice in it. It has often been urged that the surest way to lift Christianity out of the danger of assault from historical criticism is to find our one ground for certainty in experience and only in experience. But it is strangely overlooked that if historical Christianity does lie open to the attacks of historical criticism, a Christianity founded only on the inner experience of individual Christians is equally open to the attacks of the psychologists. Nothing could be more dangerous, and, in the end, more destructive to Christianity than to make it rest solely on such subjective experiences. A Christianity disentangled from the gospel facts has gotten its feet off the ground and leaped into the air and may become anything or nothing. Such Christianity has already ceased to be Christianity in any true sense of the term. To borrow an illustration: The boy playing with his kite in the windy month of March may become so sure that his kite is up for all time that he decides to cut the cord, only to find that after darting upward with unimpeded flight, it pitches headlong to the earth and lands in the mud. Says Professor A. S. Peake: "If we chafe against history as the cord which ties our soaring spirits to the earth, we are likely to find that if we snap our cord we also may plunge downward from the height it enabled us to attain."

As a matter of fact, our historical position is perfectly secure. Concerning the historical trustworthiness of our New Testament documents the following quotation from Harnack will suffice:

"There was a time—indeed, there still is for the public generally—in which the oldest Christian literature, including the New Testament, was looked upon as a tissue of forgeries and deceptions. That time is gone by. For science it was an episode in which much was learnt and after which much must be forgotten. . . . The oldest literature of the Church, whether we look at the general position or at particular details, from the historical and literary point of view, must be looked upon as trustworthy. In the whole New Testament there is probably only one book which would be classed as pseudonymous in the strictest sense of the word, and apart from gnostic forgeries, the number of pseudonymous ecclesiastical writings up to the time of Irenæus was small. . . . Also the traditions of the pre-Catholic times of literary history are in main outline trustworthy."[1]

Jesus Christ, then, stands solid in the history of our race and can no more be rooted out than the Rocky Mountains and the mighty Andes can be pulled out of the Western continent. Ernest Renan was right: You cannot any more pluck Jesus out of history than you can pluck the sun out of the heavens. And let it be understood at once that we are not now concerned with the details of historical study. For us the matter of concern is only the broad outline of New Testament facts. We are interested in the portrait of Christ. The make of the frame, the mixing of the paints, and the quality of the canvas are all quite interesting in their place. But their place is not here. At any rate, I wish to say plainly that no preacher will speak with authority who gets confused like the proverbial man who was not able to see the wood for the trees. Concerning one of our most scholarly ministers one who knew him quite well made the remark that he had devoted so much time and such meticulous care to the little things of life that he had lost the power to see the big things. And many of our technical scholars rest under this same condemnation.

I am quite sure that someone is ready now to ask: What are you going to do with the miraculous element in the gospel story? I do not overlook the importance

---

[1] Quoted in *Jesus Christ in History and Faith,* by Headlam.

of giving an answer to that question. But I turn upon you with a far more important question than that, the most important question that one man can ask another: What are you going to do with Jesus who is called Christ? I shall not permit myself to be sidetracked, neither shall I permit you to miss the main issue. The main issue is Jesus Christ. When once we have settled the question of our relation to him, then we shall be in better position to take up other and subsidiary questions.

However, with reference to the miraculous, I will say one or two things just now. I think that much of our difficulty arises out of a misunderstanding as to what we mean by "the miraculous." Unfortunately, the scientists and the theologians have been like the men working on the Tower of Babel, all laboring at the same task, but confused in speech, so that they no longer are able to understand each the other. By "the miraculous" I do not mean that God ever violates law. If he were to violate law, that would be to wreck his universe. But God is not the prisoner of the laws that he works with any more than man is a prisoner while working under law. The other remark I wish to make is this: There are no philosophical objections to the miraculous element in the gospel. Indeed, the theistic conception of the universe with its personalistic view of God, the conception upon which Christianity is based, leaves the way open for the free action of God in nature, just as certainly as the way is open for the free action of man in the world around him. Free men in the world originate things which without them would never be. They fell forests and build cities; they erect cathedrals and write poems; they paint pictures and fly in airplanes. Free men bring into being these original things. And just so, we do believe, God is free in his universe. Now the most original, and most beautiful, the most creative thing that ever came into the world was Jesus who is called the Christ. In Christ we are dealing not with a metaphysical theory; we are dealing with a mighty historic fact. It is not to be wondered at, therefore, that we read in the Gospel of certain "miracles" connected with Christ and wrought by him. This does not surprise us; the absence of such "miracles" would have been the great surprise.

But let it not be overlooked that our study in this lecture deals with Christ himself rather than anything he said or any marvelous work he is reported to have done. And in looking at Jesus we are going to strive to see him as he is. We are not going to approach the study with *a priori* notions of what he must be according to our philosophy. Rather our philosophy must be big enough to admit all the facts. The true scientist is ever ready to sit down before facts like a little child. And the scientific historian must not disregard facts in order to gain support for a preconceived view of things. By way of illustration: In his *Outline of History* H. G. Wells writes as follows: "About Jesus we have to write not theology but history, and our concern is not with the spiritual and theological significance of his life, but with its effect upon the political and everyday life of men." In criticism of Mr. Wells, let it be said that deliberately to close one's mind to the spiritual and theological significance of Jesus is not to write history at all. It is deliberately to miss the way and to fail to see the significance of Jesus. For it is the spiritual significance of his life that has affected history, and when that is left out of consideration one fails to account for history as one also fails to account for Jesus.

In this and in the following lecture I am to speak of the Christ of History and of Experience. In the present lecture I am trying to discuss the Christ of History as distinguished from the Christ of Experience. But I find that we cannot separate the one from the other, the Christ of History from the Christ of Experience, and deal with one without thinking of the other. Indeed, the two are one. It is only as Christ has value in experience that he has meaning in history. It is solely because of what Christ meant to the men of the New Testament period, that they were at pains to write down their brief memoirs of his life and to testify in their letters to churches and individuals to his significance as Saviour and Lord. And if Jesus did not still have spiritual significance for men we should be at a total loss to understand what the men of the New Testament were writing about. For spiritual things can be understood only by spiritual men.

Consider then the historical revelation of God in Christ. Now the fact of Christ is one fact, not many.

No aspect of his self-manifestation is to be separated from another and read as a thing apart. Let this be kept in the background of our thinking as we proceed.

However, there are certain features of the self-revelation of the Son of God that do stand out so distinctly as representing certain aspects of his ministry that it will be best for a time to endeavor to isolate them in our thinking and to hold them somewhat apart in our discussion. The first is the Fact of the Incarnation of God in Christ; the second is the Fact of the Crucifixion as the vivid, focal point in his atoning work, the work of bringing God and man together; the third is the Fact of the Resurrection of Christ from the Dead.

If to us men of to-day these facts have their full meaning in experience, then Christianity will have to us its full and glorious significance. But if we are not held in the grip of these facts, that is to say, if we in our own experience have not come under the power of this supreme emergence in history of the Reality at the heart of the universe, then, to say the least, we have missed some of the very best and greatest things that Christianity has to offer.

But be sure that you understand what I mean when I say these things.

I

The Incarnation of God in Christ is a fact of history. Now, as everybody knows, the word "incarnation" is just a Latin word which means—if we had any such word—"enfleshment." It signifies that in the flesh of Jesus Christ God dwelt. We must immediately get away from a doctrine that has wrought great mischief in theology—the doctrine that God and man are infinitely distant the one from the other. Let us at once discard the mischievous Gnostic notion that a long series of intermediary beings is necessary to bridge the chasm between man and the high God. And let us rid ourselves, if we can, of the deistic teaching that God stands on the outside of the world and has left it to run according to self-operating laws. Rather let us believe that "in God we live and move and have our being." Let us hold with Jesus that "My Father worketh even until now."

What the doctrine of the Incarnation really means is not that God has invaded a world that is alien to him and taken on a nature different from the divine, but rather that man and God are akin, that they belong to the same family. The doctrine of the Incarnation means that this is God's world and that history is the sphere of his activity. God and man are not unlike and totally distinct with reference to ultimate nature; they do not differ in kind. And the Incarnation of God in Christ is not altogether something new and strange, something totally different from what we see going on in the world around us all the time. Indeed, if I may so speak, God is evermore incarnating himself. He incarnates something of his beauty in a flower, something of his majesty in a storm, something of his vastness in the wide-extending sea, something of his eternity in the steadfast mountains—"God's eternities in stone." He puts something of his holiness in every saintly soul. He incarnated himself perfectly in Jesus Christ. As a matter of historical fact, *"God was in Christ."* Said Jesus, "He that hath seen me hath seen the Father." And Paul was telling what Christ had come to mean in his own experience when he wrote, "In him dwelt all the fulness of the Godhead bodily."

I have doubtless said enough already to make it plain that my own attitude toward the ancient creeds is entirely free. Let me make it clear that my attitude is not unfriendly. Before one criticizes the ancient theology and sits in judgment upon the early creeds of the Church, one would better try to understand what it was that these Church fathers were trying to say and why they were saying these things in language which now seems so strange and far away. Take the words of the great creed of Nicea which speaks of "One Lord Jesus Christ, the only begotten Son of God, begotten of the Father before all worlds, Light of Light, very God of very God, begotten, not made, being of one substance with the Father." I say it is important that we should understand what these great theologians were trying to say before we sit down to criticize them. In the long and fierce battles of the Arian controversy they saw quite plainly that the fact of the Incarnation was at stake. "Whether God was present or absent, whether the Incarnation had revealed the innermost nature of God, as written in the nature of man, or the revelation made by Christ was an official code of duty promulgated by some high celestial official"—such were the issues the fathers felt bound to settle and to settle right. "Our all is at stake," said Athanasius in justification of his lifelong conflict.

Something tremendously great and mighty had happened in history now nearly two thousand years ago. If I were to go back again to the little city by the sea where I served as pastor something like thirty years ago, and were to see cottages lifted off their foundations and moved far off from the beach, and the water line plainly on the walls of great buildings, and seaweed and shell up on the roofs of the houses, I should not need anyone to tell me that a great tidal wave had come in out of the ocean. And one has only to read history to see that about two thousand years ago a mighty tide out of the Infinite came flooding in upon our world. Everything was lifted when Jesus came. Our views of man, our thoughts about the future of human society, our outlook upon the life beyond the grave, our thoughts of God—all were lifted with the coming of Jesus. The men who saw him and had fellowship with him, saw God in him. As a calm recital of historic fact, God appeared in Christ as never before had he been seen. Out of that fact came the radiant and triumphant lives of the New

Testament Christians. Out of that experience came the New Testament itself. In Jesus God had looked upon men. These disciples had seen God in the fact of Jesus Christ. And that gave a new view of God. God and man were so close akin that God became man without man ceasing to be man and without God ceasing to be God. Out of this fact came the great creeds of the Church and notably the Creed of Nicea. Such creeds are to be understood and properly evaluated only when we appreciate the fact that strong men were in these ancient symbols trying to set forth and enable others to see and feel what they themselves had felt and seen. "These men, in a hard and brutal world of blood and steel and gold, are putting Love on the throne. They are making an affirmation not only about Christ but about the Universe. They are telling us what they believe about the very nature of things, that, in spite of all appearances, this is a Christ world."[2] These men, I say, were trying to show to others the revelation of the heart of the Father which they had seen in Jesus Christ.

This I affirm to be a fact, that God was in Christ. And this is the supreme and superlative fact of history. If one does not see God in Christ, then one will not see God anywhere. If one does truly see God in Christ, then light breaks everywhere and one has the key to the final solution of all problems in the world and out of it.

---

[2]D. S. Cairns, *The Reasonableness of the Christian Faith,* p. 175.

II

Concerning Jesus Christ the second fact is the fact of the Crucifixion as the focal point in his atoning work, his work of bringing men into fellowship with God.

I shall perhaps be told at this point that I am now mixing theory with fact, that the death of Jesus on the cross is a fact of history, but that as soon as I make use of the word "atoning" I am bringing in all sorts of theological notions. No! I am not thinking in terms of theology at all. I am making no remotest reference to any of the historic theories of the atonement. But I am saying that in a most marvelous way, as electricity diffused through the atmosphere suddenly flashes in one vivid instant across the rain cloud, so all that Christ was in his person and in his message, all that he signifies as Atoner and Redeemer, comes to a burning point in the cross.

His crucifixion, looked at from the standpoint of the casual passer-by, had to do with a cross of wood and a man nailed to it as a condemned malefactor and by the Jews considered to be accursed of God. But from the standpoint of the early Christians it was directly related to experience and came to be a mighty dynamic in their lives. And even now it can be understood, not when looked at as the passers-by looked at it, but only when seen with reference to experience. For that matter, you cannot look at the sun in the heavens as a thing merely objective and apart from all relation to experience; you can know the sun only as you know it as giving light and bathing the world in warmth. This is what I mean when I insist that the fact of having experienced the at-one-ing influences of the cross in their lives is itself a fact of history.

It is, then, a fact of history that Christ died on the cross, and that from that death on the cross in super-lative manner went influences that brought—and still do bring—God and man together. When, there-fore, the fathers said: *"Crucifixus est pro nobis sub Pontio Pilato,"* they were affirming what the cruci-fixion meant to them. *"Crucifixus est pro nobis."* It was *for us* that he was crucified. That crucifixion brought God near to them and effected a change in their thoughts of God and of their spiritual attitude toward him. And when we read certain passages in the New Testament, passages which in the very nature of the case speak the language of Jewish ritual, let us not overlook the fact that these passages came out of vital experience and had deep meaning for the men who used these ancient modes of speech. Dismiss from your minds all the long history of theological interpretation; get rid of all preconceived notions, if you can; and then take up the New Testament and read the language of experience: "The Son of man came to give his life a ransom for many," "He is the propitiation for our sins," "God was in Christ recon-ciling the world unto himself." This is not the language of theology, but the language of experienced fact.

And these great words of the New Testament vocabulary, *ransom, propitiation, reconciliation,* do have a meaning, an abiding meaning—a meaning not alone with reference to the Old Testament and Rabbinical doctrines, but also, and especially, with reference to New Testament experience. They strike the deepest note that sounds in the soul of man. They correspond to the mightiest realities with which religion has to do. And it will be the part of wisdom for us modern men not to cast out the ancient words as belonging to a dead language and conveying to us no present meaning, but rather to see if we cannot find out for ourselves what these ancient words actually do mean. And this we shall best do, not by consulting Greek lexicons and poring over learned commentaries, but by bringing to God the sacrifice of a broken and a contrite heart, and casting ourselves upon the infinite mercy of God as seen in the cross of Christ. The lexicons we shall of course study, and the commentaries we shall not neglect, but the deeper meanings of the cross reveal themselves only to the evangelical experience. And the best place to find them out is in our closet on our knees, or out in the world of want and sin where men toil and suffer and die.

And it is a noteworthy fact that within a few years after the death of Christ the temple in Jerusalem was finally destroyed and the sacrificial offerings of Jewish worshippers came to an end. "Those who looked upon

Christ's death as a sacrifice soon ceased to offer to God any bloody sacrifices at all"; and as Harnack has pointed out "wherever the Christian message subsequently penetrated the sacrificial altars were deserted and dealers in sacrificial beasts found no purchasers. If there is one thing that is certain in the history of religion it is that the death of Christ put an end to all blood sacrifice." The significance of this fact seems to lie just here: what the human heart had longed to bring about through bloody sacrifices, namely a realization of the divine presence; and what the sacrificial system of the Hebrews had in some measure accomplished, that is to say, the bringing of peace to the guilty conscience—this had been fully experienced through the supreme sacrifice in the soul of Jesus as seen in his death on the cross.

If the above presentation of the meaning of the vicarious sacrifice seems satisfactory in a very limited degree, you will permit me to remind you that the same subject will come up for further reference in the lecture immediately to follow and yet more fully in the fifth lecture, entitled, "Authority from the Cross."

III

The third and crowning fact in connection with the Incarnation is the fact of the resurrection of Christ from the dead.

It is not going too far to say that without the fact of the resurrection there would have been no New

Testament, no Christian Church, and nothing like what we now know as Christianity. The sad memory of a holy and beautiful young Galilean would doubtless long have been treasured up in hearts that loved him. Some recollections of his teachings concerning God the Father and man the child of God might have become permanently enshrined in literature. But there would have been no Christian religion in the world. Without the resurrection, the history of Christianity is simply unintelligible. Somewhere between the crucifixion and the first preaching of the disciples something happened that entirely changed their whole outlook on life and completely transformed the character of these men. Not only so, something happened that changed the history of the world. As Professor Glover says:

"The evidence for the resurrection is not so much what we read in the Gospels as what we find in the rest of the New Testament—the new life of the disciples. They are a new group. When it came to the cross, his cross, they ran away. A few weeks later we find them rejoicing to be beaten, imprisoned, and put to death. . . . We have to explain how the disciples came to conceive of another Galilean—a carpenter whom they might have seen sawing and sweating in his shop, with whom they tramped the roads of Palestine, whom they saw done to death in ignominy and derision—sitting at the right hand of God."

The story of Christ does not end with the cross. After the cross comes victory over the grave.

> "But Easter-Day breaks! But
> Christ rises! Mercy every way
> Is infinite—and who can say?"

Here, indeed, on this foundation, does Christianity stand or fall.

Let me set down in this connection the most important historical statement to be found in the entire New Testament. Here is language written by Paul, as all critics are agreed, and written within less than thirty years after the resurrection. For the student of history nothing is of equal importance with the following:

"Now I make known unto you, brethren, the gospel which I preached unto you, which also ye received, wherein also ye stand, by which also ye are saved, if ye hold fast the word which I preached unto you, except ye believed in vain. For I delivered unto you first of all that which also I received: that Christ died for our sins according to the scriptures: and that he was buried: and that he hath been raised on the third day according to the scriptures; and that he appeared to Cephas; then to the twelve; then he appeared to above five hundred brethren at once, of whom the greater part remain until now, but some are fallen asleep; then he appeared to James; then to all the apostles; and last of all, as to the child untimely born, he appeared to me also.

"Whether it be I or they, so we preach and so ye believed."[3]

---

[3] I Corinthians 15: 1-8, 11.

Now concerning this passage let a few things be specially noted:

(1) Paul declared that he delivered unto the Corinthian Christians "that which also I received." That is to say, it did not originate with him; he received it from those who had been Christians before his own conversion.

(2) His affirmation that "Christ hath been raised on the third day" harmonizes with the account of the resurrection given in the Synoptics and the Fourth Gospel. The four Evangelists all date the resurrection as having taken place on the morning of the third day. The resurrection that Paul writes about, therefore, is the resurrection that took place on the morning of the third day.

(3) Quite significant is the statement that "he appeared to above five hundred brethren at once, of whom the greater part remain until now, but some are fallen asleep." Note two things: (a) Most of the five hundred witnesses referred to were living when Paul wrote and could testify to the truthfulness of what he said. Paul's testimony, therefore, is confirmed by the most of the five hundred still living when he wrote. (b) Separate individuals, nervously disordered, do frequently see visions, but not "five hundred brethren at once." There is a proverb to the effect that "one horse may stumble at a time. But a whole stable-full at once? Impossible!"

(4) Attention should be drawn also to the concluding statement in the above-quoted passage from

Paul: "Whether then it be I or they"—the Apostle Paul or the earliest disciples of Jesus—"so we preach and so ye believed." There had seen sharp differences and disagreements between Paul and the other apostles, both personal and theological. But at no time was there any difference of opinion concerning the fact of the resurrection.

It will be seen that I am not constructing *in extenso* an argument in defense of the resurrection of Christ. I am only indicating the lines along which the fact of the resurrection must be approached. I have said nothing about the story of the Risen Christ as given in the Synoptics and John. I am aware of the fact that it is not possible to construct from these different accounts an exact and scientific narrative of the sequence of events and all their details. But I am not concerned over that. It was to be anticipated that the wonderful and unexpected appearance to his disciples of Jesus after his crucifixion would have blurred somewhat the details. This always happens in great emotional disturbances. The knowledge of the fact remains; the details are lost in the consciousness of an overwhelming reality. Besides this the evangelists were not scientific historians, they were witnesses of a mighty fact and a glorious experience. Concerning that fact in its main outlines there is no disagreement, and touching the significance and reality of the Living Christ there is uniform and convincing testimony.

I am not now going to ask the question which Paul says it is unwise to ask, namely, "How are the dead raised up? and with what body do they come?" I am satisfied with the apostle's statement, "It is sown a natural body; it is raised a spiritual body." And in our present state of philosophical and scientific knowledge—I mean our advanced state of knowledge—we may with confidence rest the question of the nature of the resurrection body just here. For with the personalists we have come to believe that the world-ground is not an inert stuff called matter, and with the physicists we have come to talk about the ultimate basis of the physical world in terms of centers of energy. This would lead us to surmise that the scientists and philosophers approaching from different sides the same problem of the ultimate nature of reality are already like workmen tunneling from opposite sides through a mountain, if they are not ready just yet to break down the thin wall still standing between them, they have at least arrived at a point where they can hear the sound of one another's pick-axes and shovels. What I mean to say is, that the question of the nature of the resurrection body is bound up with the larger question of the ultimate nature of objective reality, and at the present time philosophers and scientists are not far apart.

And I go on at once to say that all spiritually minded Christians understand that the language of the Apostles' Creed is to be taken as symbolic when we confess that Christ "ascended into heaven, and sitteth at the right hand of God the Father Almighty." For "the right hand of God the Father" is no more to be located off somewhere in space than is God himself. And God is the ever-present God. Everywhere in the Bible "the right hand" of the Lord is the symbol of his power. "His right hand, and his holy arm, hath wrought salvation for him." To be seated at the right hand of God the Father Almighty is to be in the very midst of the redemptive work which the immanent God is carrying on in the world. This is to say, wherever prison bars are being broken and the oppressed set free—there is the Living Christ; wherever burdens of sorrow are being lifted from men's shoulders and freedom and gladness given to those long bowed down under the weight of woe—there is the Living Christ; wherever men are being cleansed from sin and set in the liberty of the sons of God—there is the Living Christ; wherever the enemies of righteousness are being contended with and overthrown—there is the Living Christ. Our faith in the resurrection of Christ may, therefore, find expression in the language of the Psalmist: "Jehovah saith unto my Lord, Sit thou at my right hand until I make thine enemies thy footstool." And as the apostle says triumphantly: "He must reign till he hath put all his enemies under his feet. The last enemy that shall be abolished is death."

And this—that is to say, the faith in the Living Christ—is a fact of experience, and as we have sought to make plain, the facts of Christianity are vital only as they are or may be facts of living experience. What

I have just set forth is the uniform testimony of the saintliest souls in the Christian Church, the Church which lives through the centuries and bears testimony in the Twentieth Century as really as it did in the First Century. The life of the Church, past, present, and future, is in Christ. It continues to live because he lives. With final authority this living faith can be declared to all men everywhere. It is the faith that is being brought home to the hearts of thousands to-day with radiant certainty.

We affirm, therefore, that the only satisfactory explanation of the recovered and victorious faith of the disciples is to be found in the fact that *Jesus did objectively show himself alive to his followers after his passion*. And if I were compelled finally to say with Arthur Hugh Clough:

> "Ashes to ashes, dust to dust:
> As of the unjust, so of the just—
> *Yea of that Just One too!*
> This is the one sad gospel that is true"—

then I should feel profoundly that something had gone tremendously wrong in our universe. I therefore make the language of the New Testament my own: "Blessed be the God and Father of our Lord Jesus Christ, who begat us again unto a living hope by the resurrection of Jesus Christ from the dead."

In speaking of the authoritative basis of Christianity in history, it will be seen that we have made everything to rest upon the fact of Christ. For the

sake of clearness and emphasis we have spoken of the
Fact of the Incarnation, the Fact of the Crucifixion,
and the Fact of the Resurrection from the Dead. But
these are not separate facts; they are only three
aspects of the one supreme fact in human history—the
Fact of Christ. For the Incarnation includes the
Cross; the principle of the Cross lies at the heart of
the Incarnation; while without the triumph of the
Resurrection, all would have ended in ignominy and
shame. The Fact of Christ stands solid in the history of the world.

If now again it be objected that we have tied up
Christianity with human history, and thus laid it open
to all the assaults of historical criticism just like
any other history, we reply: Even so, what of it?
Christianity claims no special privileges. It does not
ask to be exempt from the discoveries of the
archæologists, the research of scholars, or the findings of historical critics. Christianity hates darkness;
it loves the light. It is not afraid of investigation; it
rejoices in the full blaze of the day.

It needs, moreover, to be kept in mind that Christianity is not first of all a religion of ideas; it is rather
a religion of facts. It is not first of all a religion of
ethical teachings; it is rather a religion of deeds—the
acts of God on the plane of history. Christianity,
therefore, stands or falls with its facts. As a matter of
course, the Christian religion is profoundly interested
in what Jesus said. To us he is for all time the supreme
and final teacher. Never man spake like this man.

Never will we suffer his teachings to die. But our religion is concerned supremely with what Jesus **was** and what he did. For in Christ we see God, and the acts of Jesus are the deeds of God. This is the very heart of our gospel, that in Christ God works redeemingly in the history of the world.

Furthermore, Christ does not stand in history isolated and alone. Back behind him is the long history of the Hebrew people, and after him are the New Testament, the Christian Church, and all Christian history. He can no more be detached from the history that led up to him than he can be separated from the events that follow his coming to the world. The fact of Christ must be viewed both in the light of its antecedents and of its mighty consequences. The story of Jesus fits perfectly into all the known facts. "He is not indeed the Christ that either the people or the prophets expected; but he is infinitely greater. He is a Prophet whose Divine commission has been acknowledged by great nations for many centuries; a Prince who has commanded in many lands, and for more than sixty generations, an absolute obedience and a passionate loyalty such as were never given during this brief earthly life, and within the boundaries of a single state, to the greatest of earthly sovereigns."[4]

In concluding this part of the discussion let me say that I hope it has been made plain that the major facts of history are not dependent upon the accuracy

---

[4]Dale, *The Living Christ and the Four Gospels*, p. 99.

of all minor details. Any such theory would doom us to universal historical agnosticism. We only ask that the Old Testament history be handled without prejudice and that the New Testament records be treated with scientific candor. And we rest in the confident assurance that when this is done the foundation of God will stand sure, and the Fact of Christ will be seen standing out clearly as the Light of the World. "Other foundation can no man lay than that which is laid, which is Jesus Christ."

But if these facts fail, then Christianity falls to the ground and it is all over with our religion. But in such a case we live in a crazy world where dreams are more influential than waking thoughts and fables mightier than fact, and where nothing certain can be affirmed of anything.

I hold strongly that this is a place where compromise is impossible.

V

THE BASIS OF AUTHORITY IN EXPERI-ENCE

"And it is the Spirit that beareth witness, because the Spirit is the truth."—I JOHN 5: 7.

V

THE BASIS OF AUTHORITY IN EXPERIENCE

A CONTINUALLY emerging fallacy in philosophy and theology is the interpretation of the universe in terms of the intellect alone.

Now mere intellectualism would shut us up in a very narrow world. The intellect is entirely sufficient for mathematics and chemistry and physics. But as soon as we pass into the realm of things alive the intellect halts and is blind and dumb. The True is indeed one aspect of Reality, but only *one* aspect. The Beautiful and the Good as well as the True must be taken into consideration if we would seek to know and properly to evaluate the meaning of the world. If, therefore, we seek to apprehend Reality in its totality, we must bring to it our total personality—intellect and sensibility and will.

There are many things the intellect alone can never understand. Art is of no value to the intellect. The intellect can give a chemical analysis of the paints and tell about the mechanical structure of the canvas and the frame, but the picture itself breaks away and escapes from the intellect. The intellect can tell us nothing worth while about the tear on the cheek of a child. It can indeed give the chemical analysis, it can explain the laws of physics and tell of the physiological antecedents. But the *meaning of the tear* on the cheek of a child! What does the intellect know about that? And what does the intellect know about music? The mechanics of the organ and the mathematics of harmony, and a few other inconsequential things, the intellect can explain perfectly. But the music! The *intellect knows nothing that is of æsthetic value about the music.* It is said that once when Jenny Lind was singing Dean Stanley got up and left the room. He was a man of intellect but he knew nothing about music. It was an unmeaning noise that would give a man the headache.

I

My position is that for the knowledge of God we must have not only facts of history and diagrams of doctrine presented to the mind; we must have first of all and above all the experience of God.

For that matter, without experience, the actual experience that comes from living contact with the world of men, all history whatsoever is mere annals, a narration of disconnected events in no vital relation the one to the other. Only as we are thoroughly alive in the world can we understand the world we live in.

And it must be understood, let me reiterate, that by experience we mean something more than feeling alone. Feeling is of course fundamental and the sense of value necessary to any real joy in life. But by experience of God we mean the entire self in contact with Reality. And we do not mean that in religious experience, or even in definitely evangelical experience, the emotions are always actively quickened and stirred. A constant experience of emotionalism would upset the balance and symmetry of life. The possibility of emotion is of course always present. The *religious sentiment* is always there, but not so much as "a content of consciousness" as "a feature of mental structure, a disposition to experience certain emotions on the presentation of certain ideas. These emotions are not a permanent experience of the religious man. They come and go according as the religious objects are in our mind or not. Yet the religious sentiment forms a permanent disposition toward these emotions."[1]

A recent author who discounts the value of experience and insists strongly on the scientific accuracy and finality of the Catholic creeds writes as follows: "Reason is supreme in man. To deny that Reason is the supreme arbiter in all religious questions, even in those pertaining directly to faith, is to betray the cause of religion and of philosophy, and to capitulate to the forces of superstition, fanaticism, and obscurantism."

Let me hasten to say that I fully agree that it is the worst of follies to seek to found religion upon

---

[1] Edward, *Religious Experience: Its Nature and Truth,* pp. 108, 109.

philosophical skepticism and to establish faith upon a denial of the power of the human mind to find and know the truth. But it is clear that by "reason" the author just quoted means the intellect and the intellect alone, and it is equally certain that all such systems are purely rationalistic. With the authoritarians in religion, the Creed is a correct intellectual statement of the things that must be believed, and faith is yielding intellectual assent to a system of doctrine. Hence the earnest effort to discount the value of Christian experience. And hence the following statement: "The plain man who has very little experience," but accepts everything on authority and lives a life of obedience, is "a far better Christian than his more favored brother who has a multitude of 'experiences,' on account of which he is sometimes unduly elated, and even arrogant."[2] On the contrary, we strongly insist that religion is something more than belief in certain facts of history and acceptance of certain philosophical statements written in venerable creeds, no matter how true. All this is only something external, an authority that can be imposed from without. Now such authoritarianism is most useful for building up an ecclesiasticism and holding men in subjugation, but not for the building of the kingdom of God and setting men free as the sons of God. It fails entirely to grip the heart of things. Neither facts of history nor written creeds have any power to move us fundamentally and authoritatively till inter-

---

[2] *Creeds Or No Creeds?*, pp. 135, 137.

preted and made alive in our own experience. Says the Fourth Evangelist: "This is life eternal, to know thee, the only true God and Jesus Christ whom thou hast sent." Experience is necessary if we are to have vital touch with Reality. Religion springs out of knowledge of the Living God.

I find the view which has long been mine thus expressed by Kenneth Edward:

"I am inclined to the view that in the case of religious knowledge of this order the central and inclusive intuition by which we apprehend the divine personality which is over against us is not a psychological simple, but the most highly complex and all-inclusive mental energy of which our souls are capable. It is an exercise of apprehension which occupies the whole self. It is an act which knits the entire personality together into a single apperceptive organ. The simplicity which belongs to it is not the simplicity of an isolated mental faculty, but that of a united personality gathered up into a comprehensive act of rapport."[3]

As we all know, the inductive method, the method of experiment, has created our modern science. As Bacon put it: "The question whether or no anything can be known is to be settled not by arguing, but by trying." How, by way of illustration, can we find out whether this water here on the desk before me is hot or cold? It would be a sheer waste of time to argue about it. There is only one way to find out: I

[3]*Religious Experience,* p. 208.

put my finger in it. The water is cold and not hot. I find out by trying. And how could a man living in the tropics and having no experience with freezing temperatures find out whether water will expand or contract when it freezes? If he should chance to know a little about physics, he would certainly suppose that water when solid would behave as do all other substances that he happens to be acquainted with, and that it will occupy smaller space when solid than when liquid. But if by some chance he were to happen upon zero weather, bursting pipes would apprise him of the fact that water expands when it solidifies. In physical science, *a priori* reasoning is long out of date, and it could be wished that in philosophy and religion also it might become a thing of the past.

Now religion deals primarily with matters of experience. Christianity is preëminently the religion of experience. And the way to find out the truth about religion is not by arguing, but by trying. To the question, "Can any good thing come out of Nazareth?" the answer is, "Come and see." The principle asserted by Jesus comes to the heart of the matter: "If any man willeth to do God's will, he shall know of the teaching," whether it be human and fallible, or whether it comes from God and speaks with authority to the soul of man. It is only by experiment and in experience, I say, that we can know the truth of Christianity and come into personal touch with the Living Christ. For Christian truth differs from scientific truth in this, that it is given not primarily to the intellect, not chiefly to be known intellectually, but to be lived, and to be apprehended by the total personality. And in the apprehension of it, the *conative* is of greater importance than the *cognitive*. Moral effort in the direction of Reality carries us much further in the apprehension of truth than intellectualism can ever take us.

Dr. Charles Harris, in his argument for the authoritarian view of Christianity as an intellectual system to be interpreted in terms of the Aristotelian philosophy, affirms that "from experience it cannot even be known that Jesus ever existed." He writes:

"If we reflect how we know that a person called Jesus of Nazareth once lived and died upon the cross, we perceive at once that we know it, not from experience, but from the two sources of (1) oral tradition, and (2) certain ancient books, especially the books of the New Testament. By a process of logical inference from these two sources of information, we reach the conclusion that Jesus once lived a human life upon earth."[4]

And he goes on to say:

"Even if it is conceded that his existence was once a matter of direct experience to his contemporaries living in Palestine, yet certainly it is not a matter of direct experience to anyone now."

Somehow, these words do not satisfy us. They leave something out. They do not present a Christ

---

[4] *Creeds Or No Creeds?*, p. 133.

who is alive; they give us only a written description of him. They do not offer us the music—not a note of music is sounding; they give us only the printed sheet on which are written certain curious-looking characters. Indeed, such a Christianity is not the Christianity of the New Testament. It is not *life,* but *law;* not fellowship with a Living Person, but obedience to an ecclesiasticism; not experience of the Divine, but assent to an intellectual formula.

We agree, therefore, with Dr. Garvie:

"Surely if the historical Jesus has the significance and value for the race which is generally accorded Him, it is a justifiable conclusion that His relation to it should become universal and permanent, not in a less immediate and influential form than in the days of His flesh. If He be the Word of God become flesh, the Son revealing the Father, if He be the Saviour who died for us, and whose death atones for sin, it is reasonable to believe that He always and everywhere Himself reveals God and redeems man. The denial of the fellowship of the Christian with the Living Christ is reasonable only if He is not at all what Christian faith claims Him to be."[5]

Our contention is that History and Experience cannot be separated the one from the other and that the Christ of History is also the Christ of Experience. The basis of authority in Christianity is not where it has usually been sought—in an infallible Church, or in an infallible creed, or in an infallible

[5]*Christian Certainty,* pp, 219, 220.

Bible. The final authority is to be found in the Christ of History who is the Christ of Experience—not in the Christ of Experience alone, nor alone in the Christ of History, but in the Christ of History who is the Christ of Experience. Here do we find ultimate certitude.

And it is seen at once that the sort of authority we are talking about is of a different order from that which has been insisted upon by those who are more interested in ecclesiastical institutions and intellectual systems, than they seem to be in a Christlike life and in a satisfying experience.

II

And now in the paragraphs that immediately follow one is compelled to speak modestly. I would not dare to lay claim to experiences about which I know nothing. But one would be false to a trust if one did not speak out the things whereby one lives.

Now none of the great things of the spirit flaunt themselves in the faces of men. They do not strive nor cry, neither do they lift up the voice in the street. Sometimes they are but as a whisper out of the Infinite and often as a still small voice which is even less than a whisper. The present lecturer does not dare to count himself among the saints nor claim anything more than a distant kinship with the High Order of Mystics. And yet their language is not wholly a foreign and unknown tongue, and when he listens to the great saints holding high converse one with another, he catches a sentence here and there that is understood, and what is understood shakes the soul with a strange emotion and compels him to feel that he has touched at last the essence of Reality.

In the things I am now about to say I am not writing as an individual. I am speaking in a representative capacity. What I am saying about the meaning and value of Christ in experience is said out of the experience of Christian men in all ages and in all lands. But I do affirm that I also know the meaning of the words that follow:

(1) It is affirmed then that the Christian does have personal knowledge of Christ as Lord.

In the beginning this came to men as a truth of experience. Said Paul: "No man can say that Jesus is Lord but by the Holy Spirit." Here is both theology and religion. The affirmation, "Jesus is Lord"—that is theology. The experience through the Holy Spirit which enables one to say, "Jesus is Lord"—that is religion. The doctrine simply gives intellectual expression to what Christ is felt to be. Jesus had revealed God in the experience of the early Christians and had become Lord of their lives before they set down any doctrine of the divinity of Christ. And with us at the present time it is only as one has had experience of Christ as Lord and Saviour that to him the doctrine of the divinity of Christ has any meaning.

And furthermore, in the very nature of the case, the doctrine of the divinity of Christ is a truth that can be proved only to the soul that has had experience of Christ. It is only as one finds God in Christ that one bows before him as Lord. I think that much valuable time is often wasted trying to convince men by the wrong method. For instance, I do not think any progress is made by bringing forward evidence to prove that Christ was born of a virgin, and that therefore he was the Son of God. For it is conceivable that one might have been born of a virgin and yet be less than the Son of God. He might be an angel or a superman, and nothing more. Do not misunderstand me; I myself raise no question touching the historical trustworthiness of the accounts of the Virgin Birth of our Lord. I have always felt that no more beautiful and appropriate way could be imagined for the realization of the Wonder of the Incarnation. And I think it will be agreed that the story of the Virgin Birth has through history served as a kind of protecting envelope for the doctrine of the Incarnation of the Son of God. But you cannot prove the divinity of Christ by the Virgin Birth. It is the divinity of Christ that has made it easy for devout souls through the centuries to accept the stories given in Matthew and Luke as indicating truly the wonderful manner in which the Incarnation was realized.

Nor do I think that by any other entirely intellectual process you will be able to convince the mind with reference to the divinity of our Lord. You can easily prove that he was the greatest of all the prophets. You will have no difficulty in getting people to agree that spiritually he was the tallest of all the sons of men. I think these methods are useful. They carry us pretty far in the right direction. But they all stop short of the goal. They miss the great objective.

My point is that something more than the intellect is needed if one is to rest in the assurance that God was incarnate in Christ. What I am saying is that only in Christian experience can Christ be fully known. If therefore the proverbial man in the street or the philosopher in his chair in the university raises questions touching the divinity of Christ, there is but one answer to be given: Open your heart to him. Surrender to him as the highest and best this world has ever seen. Expose your soul to him and let him have his way with you, and then his authority will assert itself. His authority is the final authority of the spiritual. It is an authority that vindicates itself. In the realm of the moral he is ultimate. To quote Dr. Dale:

"If you have found in Christ the supreme and ultimate authority over your moral and spiritual life, you have found God in him. If you have found in Christ the infinite mercy of God, you have found God in him. If you have found in Christ the Giver and Source of perpetual support and defense of that divine life which renders righteousness and saintliness possible in this world, you have found God in him."

"It is not because we first believe that he is divine that we acknowledge his authority over our moral and religious life; it would be truer to say that in discovering his authority, we discover that he is divine."[6]

According to the view here presented, Christ is brought into the same relation to believing men to-day as he bore to his disciples in the days of his flesh. His life and his works brought home to their experience the reality of the divine power that dwelt in him. And still to-day as of old, the facts of his life and death and resurrection and the presence of his Spirit abiding in the world convince men that he is the Son of God. Our faith in him is in response to his presence and is the result of his power. Thus it appears that the Christ of History is the Christ of Experience.

(2) And what shall we say about the cross of Christ in Christian experience? I call attention to the fact that in the experience of Christian men the forgiveness of sins is directly related to the death of Christ. His crucifixion is the ultimate manifestation of the suffering love of God. And this manifestation is validated in Christian experience.

No one sentence in the New Testament more certainly sets forth the meaning of Christ in the experience of men than those words in the Fourth Gospel: "Behold, the Lamb of God, that taketh away the sin of the world!" Bunyan's immortal story of the Christian pilgrim is far more than a transcript of his own Puritan experience. It tells the story of every

---

[6]*Christian Doctrine,* pp. 110, 120.

distinctly evangelical experience, and never with profounder discernment than in his account of what took place at the sight of the cross:

"He ran thus till he came at a place somewhat ascending, and upon that place stood a cross, and a little below, in the bottom, a sepulchre. So I saw in my dream, that just as Christian came up with the cross, his burden loosed from his shoulders, and fell from off his back, and began to tumble, and so continued to do, till it came to the mouth of the sepulchre, where it fell in, and I saw it no more. . . . Then Christian gave three leaps for joy and went on singing."

Let that be specially noted: *"Then Christian gave three leaps for joy and went on singing."* The songs of the Christian Church have come ringing down the centuries from the first days until now. We turn to one of the earliest books in the New Testament and we hear the song: "Unto him that loveth us, and loosed us from our sins in his own blood; and he made us to be a kingdom, to be priests unto his God and Father; to him be the glory and the dominion forever and ever." And we turn also to one of the hymns of the Church of to-day, and still we hear the same glad strain:

"When I survey the wondrous cross
    On which the Prince of glory died,
My richest gain I count but loss,
    And pour contempt on all my pride.

"Forbid it, Lord, that I should boast,
    Save in the death of Christ, my God;
All the vain things that charm me most,
    I sacrifice them to his blood.

"See from his head, his hands, his feet,
    Sorrow and love flow mingled down!
Did e'er such love and sorrow meet,
    Or thorns compose so rich a crown?

"Were the whole realm of nature mine,
    That were a present far too small;
Love so amazing, so divine,
    Demands my soul, my life, my all."

Nothing is deeper in the experience of Christian men than is the cross of Christ. But about this we shall speak more at length in the succeeding lecture.

(3) And I affirm also that the Christ of our faith is not dead, but alive forever.

When we speak here of the Living Christ we intend that our words should be understood as meaning what they say. We mean that the Christ who lived and died is alive forevermore. And the best of Christians through all the centuries have borne witness to fellowship with Him. As we have seen, the Resurrection of Christ from the dead does stand as one of the great objective facts of history—not as an hallucination, but as a fundamental datum of historic Christianity. The fact of the resurrection has indeed been established by "many infallible proofs." But suppose that the evidence for the resurrection had been more cogent still, that Christ had been seen in bodily form not by his followers alone, but by his enemies also. Suppose that the evidence for his coming alive out of the grave had been such that all historians without exception had accepted the fact of the resurrection just as all accept the fact of Cæsar or Napoleon or Washington. I mean to say, suppose that the rising from the dead of the crucified Jesus had been a mere fact of ancient history, having no direct relation to living Christian experience. What then? Then I submit that the whole story of the world would have been other than it is. I submit that the New Testament would not have been written and that the Christian Church would have been nonexistent. For it was the experience of the Living Christ that gave birth to the Church.

Read the story as we have it in the New Testament. One can see perfectly what was going on in those beginning days of the Church. First there ran the amazing story that Jesus had risen from the dead. Then two disciples reported that they had seen him on the road to Emmaus and that he had been made known to them as the bread was broken. Then others reported that they had seen him alive. But he came and went. He appeared for a little while and then was gone again. They were as yet bewildered and frightened. Then something tremendously great happened. The Day of Pentecost came. What was the significance of Pentecost? How was it that after the experience of that day, all fear departed and perfect confidence reigned? What happened on Pentecost?

Leave out of consideration all the strange occurrences connected with the account of that day and come to the heart of the matter. On that mighty day the disciples came to the full confidence that Jesus was alive forever. On that day he came and he never went away again. During the wonderful forty days he had come and gone; he had been with them and then he departed from them. But henceforth, following the Day of Pentecost, Christ was with them all the time.

I submit, then, that it is because of the experience of the Living Christ in the lives of men that the Church will not let die the wonderful story of Easter morning.

> "And not for signs in heaven above
>   Or earth below they look;
> Who know with John His smile of love,
>   With Peter His rebuke.
>
> "In joy of inward peace, or sense
>   Of sorrow over sin,
> He is his own best evidence,
>   His witness is within.
>
> "No fable old, nor mythic lore,
>   Nor dream of bards and seers,
> No dead fact stranded on the shore
>   Of the oblivious years.
>
> "But warm, sweet, tender, even yet
>   A present help is he;
> And faith has still its Olivet,
>   And love its Galilee.

III

We are well aware that objections to the argument from experience will come flocking in at once. We are prepared to meet them.

(1) And first let it be kept in mind that we have found our basis of ultimate authority, not in the Christ of Experience alone, but in the Christ of Experience and of History.

Christianity is securely anchored in history. It was the peculiar merit of Ritschl that he related Christian experience directly to Christian history. Ritschl was obsessed with an aversion to mysticism and he was handicapped with the supposed distinction between the noumenal and the phenomenal. We cannot follow him at either of these points. But the real merit of his system is here where he insists that faith and fact must go hand in hand. Ritschl's doctrine of value judgments has been most fruitful; we appreciate its importance and have been greatly aided by it in our thinking. But value judgments are not to be dissociated from historical fact. As Harnack states it: "The whole substance and meaning of religion, life in God, the forgiveness of sins, consolation in suffering—the Church couples with Christ's person; and in so doing she associates everything that gives life its meaning and its permanence, nay, the Eternal itself, with an historical fact, maintaining the indissoluble unity of both."[7] Christian faith, thus keep-

---

[7] Quoted in Garvie's *The Ritschlian Theology*, p. 219.

ing her feet firmly planted on facts of history, is not in danger of drifting off into the air.

(2) It may be objected that the experience of Christians herein discussed is wholly subjective and of no value for objective knowledge.

(a) This objection comes first from those who insist that Christianity rests securely only on authority to be enforced from without, that it is a creed to be accepted and a law to be obeyed.

An Anglo-Catholic critic puts his objection to the argument from experience in the following words: "They contend that they are aware of the existence of Jesus, because of the grace they receive when they pray to him, or to God through him, which grace is to them a matter of experience. But experience of grace received only yields knowledge that grace is received, not knowledge of the source from which it is derived." One is surprised that the objector does not press his criticism just a little further and go on to deny that in experience one knows "that grace *is* received." For if one cannot trust his experience of Christ, how can one trust his experience of "grace"? What is this thing called "grace," anyhow? We see coming to the front just here the curious notion of "grace" as a sort of Fourth Person in the Holy Trinity. "Grace" is here objectified and made an *entity,* just as the deist objectifies "law" and turns over to *law* the deeds of the ever-present God. We insist that in experiencing "grace" one comes into personal touch with God.

(b) This same objection comes also from our new school of psychologists. We feel confident that the deductions from the findings of the psychologists have gone entirely too far. Many psychologists seem to have reached the conclusion that a description of behavior is equivalent to a theory of causation. And some of the rest of us have been all too quick in following their lead. Take, for instance, the following quotation from a delightful volume of religious essays only recently from the press: "The heart of man persistently turns to the desire for immediate communion with God. A critical philosophy assures him that what he conceives as an immediate knowledge of God is only an immediate knowledge of his own experience which he interprets by reference to a supposed objective reality. This criticism of mysticism," the writer quoted goes on to say, "is to my mind quite valid."[8]

To the mind of the present lecturer, this criticism is not valid at all. The trouble with it is that it goes too far. For when once you are logical and thorough in the application of it, you sweep away the foundations of all knowledge, and land us in nothing but "an immediate knowledge of our own experience" *with reference to everything*. With reference to knowledge of any supposed objective reality, of what, as a matter of fact, are we really conscious, say, with

---

[8]Garrison, *Affirmative Religion*, p. 232.

reference to the chapel in which we are assembled, or the audience here present, or the sheet of paper from which I am now reading? Might we not with equal truth say, "What he conceives as knowledge of the chapel, and the audience, and the manuscript is only knowledge of his own experience which he interprets by reference to a supposed objective reality?" It must be evident at once that any such critical philosophy lands us immediately in *solipsism*. The only thing such a philosopher could be perfectly sure of would be *himself,* and upon closer analysis there would presently be seen cogent reasons for questioning even that. It seems rather strange, therefore, that this "fallacy of psychologism" should not be immediately recognized. If this argument holds against our experience of Christ as discussed above, it ought to hold equally against our experience of our fellow men: and it seems that there is no good reason why it should not hold against all knowledge of the objective world.

We therefore reiterate our position that the ultimate source of all knowledge is in experience. Take the knowledge of God, by way of illustration. How did men come to believe in God? They did not sit down to prove that God is. Our historic arguments —*ontological, cosmological, teleological*—all came in after faith had arrived and were attempts to justify that faith. Faith was originally the response of the soul to the ever-present God, or let me say the answer of the child to the call of the Father. As Tennyson puts it:

> "Here sits he shaping wings to fly:
> His heart forbodes a mystery:
> He names the name Eternity.

> "The type of Perfect in his mind
> In Nature he can nowhere find,
> He sows himself on every wind.

> "He seems to hear a Heavenly Friend,
> And through thick veils to apprehend
> A labour working to an end."

We hold, then, that if we are ready to trust the report of the objective world that comes to us at second hand through the channel of the five senses, there can be no reason why we should doubt the testimony of the personality in its totality when the soul stands face to face with God.

(3) And it must not be forgotten that the Christian experience we have been discussing is not merely the experience of one man, nor of a few, but the experience of a multitude of men and women from the earliest days of the Christian Church even down to the present hour.

Certain individuals such as Mahomet, Joan of Arc, and Joseph Smith have seen visions and heard voices. But we know how to classify all such auditions and visions. They were wholly subjective; they did not correspond to any objective reality. They were their own; they were not shared by others. "A man's private illusions are his own. If other men see what he sees, hear what he hears, feel what he feels, taste what he tastes, he may dismiss the fear that his organs are unsound."

What we have, then, in the experience of Christians is the collective consciousness of an innumerable company of witnesses. If, by way of illustration, we were to go out to-night and stand under the star-lit heavens and I were to insist that in the southern sky there was shining a great red star, my friends would take me by the arm and send me to the hospital. But if to-night we go out and look up at the northern heavens and I ask if you see the North Star, at once comes the answer that you do. Hundreds of us see the North Star at one and the same time. Throughout the centuries men have been looking up at the North Star. Paul, David, Abraham—all saw that star. And when first men stood out under the stars and wondered and adored and worshipped, that star was shining there. There can be no doubt about it—that North Star is more than a subjective experience; it is an objective reality. And just so with the testimony touching the validity of our experience concerning the spiritual universe. The Epistle to the Hebrews thus speaks of it: Abel "had witness borne to him"; Enoch "had witness borne to him"; and Noah and Abraham and Isaac and Jacob and Joseph and Moses and a long line of heroes and martyrs—"these all had witness borne to them" of the everlasting reality of our holy religion. The New Testament Christian, looking back over Old Testament history, sees that he is "compassed about with a great cloud of witnesses" to the reality of the spiritual world. Exactly so, we Christians of the Twentieth Century, looking back over our Christian history, see a cloud of witnesses—Phillips Brooks and Jonathan Edwards and John Wesley and John Knox and John Calvin and Martin Luther and Augustine, and the Apostle Paul—all testifying to what they had felt and seen. Moreover, we are now living in fellowship with multitudes of Christian people who bear witness to the same thing.

(4) Nevertheless, to refer to our illustration about the "red star," that red star might as a matter of fact be there shining in the southern heavens. The man who insists that it is there might turn out to be right and all the others wrong. For he might have better eyes than they or he might have some gift of sight peculiar to himself. And pioneers, whether in the field of science or in the sphere of religion, have always been solitary and lonely men. For there is deep kinship between the method of religion and the method of science. Men of science and men of religion both move forward by making the venture of faith. The True is only one aspect of Reality, but it is one aspect, and he who ventures out to discover Truth is on his way in search of God. Moreover, the fidelity of men of science to Truth at any cost may well stand as an example to the men whose chief

interest is in religion. And many a scientist has had to wait a long time for others with less power of insight to catch up with him.

And it is precisely so with religion. There would have been no Christian faith in the world to-day had it not been for lonely men who ran ahead of the rest of the race and saw what only the eye of faith can see. Abraham was "the friend of God" while all around him wondered at his folly. Moses saw a bush ablaze with the divine presence and heard a voice calling him to rescue Israel from bondage, while those around him saw only the stunted growth of the wilderness and heard nothing more than the familiar sounds of the desert. Elijah heard a "still small voice," while nobody else heard anything more than the wind and the earthquake. Saul of Tarsus on the road to Damascus, while those who journeyed with him stood still and could make nothing of the strange confusion, saw the Living Christ and received the command that changed the direction of his life and influenced profoundly the entire history of our western world. The Epistle to the Hebrews, after calling over the names of men of old who dared to follow the vision that lured them on, calls upon all Christians to be encouraged by their example and to press forward, looking unto "Jesus the pioneer and the perfection of faith."[9] Jesus is indeed the perfect example of the daring of faith, and in a peculiar sense he is

[9]Moffatt's translation.

faith's "pioneer." He passed over into new realms of experience. He explored vast regions hitherto unknown. And he leads the way to the realization of the full meaning of the ultimate Reality. Following him we shall find God. Let us dare, therefore, to listen to the voice that sounds in our own souls and never be disobedient to "the heavenly vision."

(5) There is yet one other thing to be said: Christian experience bears fruit in Christlike living. "By their fruits ye shall know them."

Christian experience is thus far more than mere *emotionalism.* To think of it chiefly as emotionalism is to misunderstand the whole matter. Christian experience has in it a *noetic quality;* it brings the soul into touch with a spiritual world which is everlastingly real. Also Christian experience has in it a *moral quality.* It comes as a consequence of a striving in the direction of the ethical ideal; it is crowned by a new birth within the soul of qualities that are forever beautiful and good. Although William James, in his *Varieties of Religious Experience,* is dealing almost exclusively with the eccentric and neurotic, nevertheless, as a result of his studies, he has this to say: "The best fruits of religious experience are the best things that history has to show. They have always been esteemed so; here if anywhere is the genuinely strenuous life; and to call to mind a succession of such examples as I have lately had to wander through, though it has been only in reading of them, is to feel encouraged and uplifted and washed in better moral air."[10]

Religious experience, and especially the more definitely Christian experience unquestionably does have a life value and validates itself in ethical action. It ministers to life; it constructs personality; it makes an enormous contribution to the moral power of the race. In Christian experience energy to live by does actually come into the lives of men. "The universe backs the experience."[11]

The Christ of History does truly become the Christ of Experience, and thus the "first born among many brethren." Thus testified the apostle: "It is no longer I that live, but Christ liveth in me: and the life which I now live in the flesh I live in faith, the faith which is in the Son of God, who loved me and gave himself up for me."

Thus it has come about that Christian experience bearing fruit in Christlike lives is the crowning evidence of the truth of the Christian religion; "for the gospels are not four, but 'ten thousand times ten thousand, and thousands of thousands,' and the last word in every one of them is, 'Lo, I am with you alway, even unto the end of the world.' "[12]

If, then, we inquire where the ultimate basis of authority in religion is to be found, we make answer:

---

[10]James, *Varieties of Religious Experience,* p. 259.

[11]See Jones, *Studies in Mystical Religion,* p. xxx.

[12]Glover, *The Conflict of Religions in the Early Roman Empire,* p. 140.

Not where ecclesiastics and theologians have been looking for it, but just here in *History* and in *Experience*—in Experience verifying History and in History informing Experience. Not in History alone nor in Experience alone do we find the basis of authority in religion, but in History and in Experience.

VI

AUTHORITY FROM THE CROSS

"And I, if I be lifted up from the earth, will draw all men unto myself."—JOHN 12: 32.

VI

AUTHORITY FROM THE CROSS

THE Catholic Church exercises its vast power and influence over the lives of its devout communicants chiefly through their faith in "the miracle of the Eucharist" and in "the power of the keys."

The Eucharist is the central and supreme act of worship in sacrementarian churches. The dogma is that when the officiating priest lifts up the bread and chalice repeating the words, "This is my body . . . This is my blood," the bread and the wine are actually changed into the very body and blood of Christ. When the communicant, therefore, eats the wafer he takes Christ's very body into his mouth. The adoration of the Host naturally follows. The "miracle" having taken place, a bell is rung and before the elevated Host the priest and congregation bend the knee and worship. The influence of this ceremony over devout Catholics who believe that Christ's body broken on the cross is thus visibly before them can hardly be overestimated.

Second to this in importance is the priest's power of absolution, his power to pronounce the forgiveness of sins. Some months ago the daily press carried a story of a Catholic priest who had invited a family of friends to be his guests on an excursion boat on one of the Great Lakes. A sudden accident having happened, they were about to sink to their death in the water when, calling them to him, the priest held before them his crucifix and in the language of the ritual of his church pronounced the forgiveness of sins. One gladly confesses to a thrill of admiration at his heroism, and one does not doubt that their faith, his and theirs, met with its eternal reward.

What I wish to emphasize is the fact that in spite of what we believe to be superstition and error, the Catholic Church secures and keeps its strong hold over millions of devout souls through its belief and practice with reference to the perpetual meaning of the broken body of Christ and the forgiveness of sins. Thus the Catholic Church does bring satisfaction to the deepest human needs.

And if human needs are to be satisfied these two things must forever be kept before the minds of sinful men—the cross of Christ and the gospel of the divine forgiveness. For here in the cross is found what is central and distinctive in our religion. The atoning death of Christ and the forgiveness of sins is the final authoritative gospel that the Christian preacher has to announce to men.

Professor A. V. G. Allen, in *The Continuity of Christian Thought,* writes as follows:

"The absence of preaching is one of the striking features of the mediæval Church. . . . The sacramental theology dispenses with the necessity of preaching, for it professes to accomplish the end of preaching in another way. . . . Wycliffe showed his sense of its value by organizing his band of preachers to go throughout the kingdom proclaiming the gospel as it was then read in all its freshness and novelty in the newly translated Bible. . . . All the pomp and splendor of the Church and its ritual were as nothing compared with the fascination which the people felt under the spell of the preacher. . . . When the Reformation was accomplished, it took its rightful place in the newly constituted churches, becoming, as it were, the sacrament of the larger faith."[1]

In our Protestant churches, then, let it be said at once, the preaching of the gospel of the cross is the sacrament of the larger faith.

In churches where the sacramental theory prevails it is not the sermon that is of first importance but the sacrament, and therefore the place of first importance is given to the altar. But the pulpit is the altar of our Protestant churches. Here, by the preacher in the sermon, Christ is lifted up and all men are drawn unto him. What the miracle of the Eucharist is supposed to do, that the presentation of Christ in preaching by men who truly know him in the forgiveness of sins actually does in churches of the evangelical faith. And let it be emphasized that the pulpit is not a lecture platform where just any and every thing may be discussed. And certainly the pulpit is not an open forum where anything or nothing may be affirmed. The lecture platform is useful and the

---

[1]Allen, *The Continuity of Christian Thought*, pp. 251, 252.

open forum serves a valuable purpose. But the pulpit is not the place for either. The business, the privilege, the high calling of the preacher is to present Christ and him crucified, and with Paul the modern preacher might well exclaim, "Woe is me if I preach not the gospel!"

In one of Tennyson's letters there is a delightful story. The poet had arrived at an inn kept by "two perfectly honest Methodists." Upon greeting them he asked for the news of the day. "Why, Mr. Tennyson," said his hostess, "there's only one piece of news that I know, that Christ died for sinners." "Well," answered Tennyson, "that is old news and good news and new news." This is indeed the good news, the glad tidings to sinful men—that Christ died for sinners. This is the "word" that Paul exhorted Timothy to preach: "Preach the Word." This is the "word" to which the apostles said they must give themselves: "It is not fit that we should forsake the word of God and serve tables." This is the sum and substance of Christian preaching: "the word of life," "the word of the cross," "the word of reconciliation," "the word of salvation."

And it cannot be questioned that according to the writers of the New Testament this is the very heart of the gospel. Take, for instance, Christ's farewell instructions as given in the Gospel according to Luke: "Then opened he their mind, that they might understand the scriptures; and he said unto them, Thus it is written, that the Christ should suffer, and rise again from the dead on the third day; and their repentance and remission of sins should be preached in his name unto all the nations, beginning from Jerusalem. Ye are witnesses of these things." That is to say, the offer of repentance and remission of sins was based on the fact of the sufferings and resurrection of Christ.

One great word from Paul will be in place here and will suffice: "But all things are of God, who reconciled us to himself through Christ, and gave unto us the ministry of reconciliation; to wit, that God was in Christ reconciling the world unto himself, and having committed to us the world of reconciliation." And so say all the men of the New Testament. The most characteristic thing about Christianity is the cross. Christianity might conceivably give up something—yes, many things—and still be essentially Christian. But if we ever give up the cross, whatever else may remain, it will not be the religion of the New Testament—*and the only hope of the world will be gone.*

Professor T. R. Glover, in his delightful little book *The Jesus of History,* writing of the Christian Church in the Roman Empire, raises the question how it came about that in so short a time the early Christian Church was able to overcome the pagan religion, the official religion of the Roman Empire, with all its antiquity, splendor, and power. He answers: "The Christian out-lived the pagan, out-died him, and out-thought him." To this illuminating analysis one would find it necessary to add a fourth reason—and the supreme reason: *The Christian preached the forgiveness of sins through faith in Jesus' blood.* "Christianity conquered through its message that in Jesus there is personally present a God who receives sinners. It triumphed not because it was the religion most hospitable to fresh ideas, not merely because its moral and social doctrine was of a higher character than its rivals, or because it was the faith best fitted to win educated minds. It is the new element in a faith that tells, and Christianity overcame by means of its message of forgiveness, in which it had no rival."[2] As the Seer of Patmos put it: "And they overcame by the blood of the Lamb, and by the word of their testimony, and they loved not their lives unto the death."[3]

I

Let us ask then: How is the death of Christ related to salvation from sin?

We shall seek to answer this question in language that has meaning in experience. We recognize that all language is symbolic, and supremely so when it deals with spiritual things. If only this had been generally understood it would have fared better with theology. And if now we are ready to recognize it, we shall make larger use of New Testament terms in sincerer appreciation of the fact that they are fluid and poetic and not fixed and scientific.

---

[2]Mackintosh, *The Christian Experience of Forgiveness*, p. 21.
[3]Rev. 12:11.

A story told of Horace Bushnell is in point. One day when a friend asked him why it was that he complained that his critics had misunderstood him, and why he did not express himself more clearly so that others would not misapprehend his position, he gave this answer:

"It is because of the different views which they and I take of the human soul and of the relation of language to spiritual truth. They succeed easily in so expressing their ideas as to be understood by their readers; but it is because they deal with subjects mechanically, and not according to nature. There, for instance, is Dr. ——, my customary assailant. He writes about the human spirit as if it were a machine under the laws of mechanics; and of course what he says is perfectly intelligible, like any other treatise on matter; only what he says is not true! But I conceive of the soul in its living nature—as free, and intelligent, and sensitive; as under vital and not mechanical laws. Language, too, for that reason, is not so much descriptive as suggestive, being figurative throughout, even where it deals with spiritual truth. Therefore an experience is needed to interpret words."[4]

We preachers of the Twentieth Century have fallen heir to theories of the atonement, methods of expression, forms of words, that were useful enough in their day, and in their time did speak to men in language they could understand. But these forms of expression do not appeal to us any longer. The notion

---

[4] T. T. Munger's *Horace Bushnell*, pp. 107, 108.

of a ransom to the devil, the theory of a penal sub-
stitution, the moral influence theory, were all efforts
to explain the mightiest deed in the moral history of
the race. But they do not satisfy us now. And in the
general break-up in modern theological thinking no
great doctrine suffered quite so much as did the doctrine of the cross. As a result there has been a let-
down in the "preaching of the cross." Preachers became uncertain and confused just where they needed
most to be clear-eyed and authoritative. But I think
this was only a passing phase and that it is not true
any longer. We have come now to interpret all things
in terms of life. I think that now, as not in many years,
the doctrine of the cross is sounding forth from our
pulpits in language that reaches and stirs the hearts
of people.

We cannot speak of the death of Jesus as we
would speak of the death of any ordinary man. For
Jesus was no ordinary man. Christ is the manifestation of the moral quality of Reality. We cannot
avoid the conviction that he is the Moral Absolute,
that God did come to perfect moral self-expression
in Jesus. The death of Jesus, therefore, is the revelation of the heart of God. God is nowhere so fully
disclosed as in the death of Christ. All that Jesus
came to teach and to do comes to a focus, to a burning point, in the cross. Thus the cross becomes the
supreme symbol of our religion. There is of course
mystery in the cross, but it is not mystery that is darkness at the core, but mystery that is full of light.

"All the light of sacred story
Gathers round its head sublime."

Briefly, then, let me make several suggestions touching the meaning of the cross.

(1) The death of Jesus shows what it cost God to save men from sin.

Sin is the central evil of the world. Sorrow and death are companion evils. Sin, sorrow, and death —these are the age-old enemies of man. These seem, in hours of solemn thought, to negative all things we have to say about the goodness and mercy of God. Death shuts down like an icy slab upon all that we love. Sorrow soon or late comes to every man and breaks his heart. Now "the sting of death is sin," and the sting of sorrow also is sin. Sin lies at the root of the tragedies of life and of death. Christianity is the only religion in the world that fully acknowledges the presence and power of sin in the world, and undertakes to enter into conflict with it, promising men to deliver them from it. Other religions take different attitudes. They accept evil as a fact and hold that the struggle between Light and Darkness must go on forever; or they take the position that evil is illusion or error of mortal mind and deny and ignore it; or they fail to see that the fundamental human problem is the moral problem and occupy themselves with other things. But Christianity sees into the heart of things and recognizes that the root evil of all evils is sin. And then Christianity goes forward to offer a way of escape, a method of deliverance. Christianity does not coldly say with Emerson, "The dice of God are always loaded. Every secret is told, every crime is punished, every virtue rewarded, every wrong redressed in silence and certainty. What we call retribution is the universal necessity by which the whole appears wherever a part appears." No, we are not bound up in a world of fixed fate. Christianity does not silently submit to things as they are, hypnotizing itself with the theory that everything is exactly as it ought to be. The terrible facts of life are here— sin and sorrow and death—and Christianity sees them and enters into battle with them.

Here is the sublime significance of the cross of Christ. In the work and teaching of Jesus we see God drawing near to men and speaking in their language. In the cross of Christ we see the battle at its climax. For God does not sit apart from men and from remote spaces look down on human sin and sorrow. He comes all the way to our actual situation and deals with us as we actually are. He enters into companionship with us. He takes our sins and sorrows home to himself and makes them a part of the divine experience, and by so doing he redeems us.

> "It is by no breath,
> Turn of eye, wave of hand, that salvation joins issue
>   with death."

It is rather by personal, hand-to-hand struggle that God in Christ wins the victory over evil, so that before he ascends to the Father he is able to call to his disciples, "In the world ye shall have tribulation; but be of good cheer; I have overcome the world."

(2) The cross of Christ is the revelation of the way God has, from the beginning of time, been carrying the burden of the world's sorrow.

With marvelous power of insight does the Apocalypse speak of Christ as "the Lamb slain from the foundation of the world." The principle of vicarious suffering, the fact of perpetual sin-bearing, is eternal in the innermost life of God. To quote Principal Fairbairn:

"Sin was, as it were, the sorrow in the heart of His happiness. Theology has no falser idea than that of the impassibility of God. If He is capable of sorrow, He is capable of suffering; and were He without the capacity of either, He would be without any feeling of the evil of sin or the misery of man. But to be passible is to be capable of sacrifice; and in the presence of sin the capacity could not but become the reality. The being of evil in the universe was to God's moral nature an offense and a pain, and through His pity the misery of man became His sorrow. We may, then, construe the sufferings and death of Christ as if they were the sacraments, or symbols and seals, of the invisible passion and sacrifice of the Godhead."[5]

Now my position is not that God has from the beginning been passively bearing the sorrow of the world on his heart, and standing aside as a silent

---

[5] *The Place of Christ in Modern Theology*, pp. 483-485.

sufferer. *The cross of Christ is the revelation of the way God has been dealing with sin all the time.* The suffering love of God is not an isolated event. It is not an eddy in the main current of history. It is far more than an episode in the evolution of the eternal ages. What Christ did on the cross, God is always doing. God himself enters upon the field of battle. Nay, he has always been in the midst of the fight. He undertakes the battle on our behalf. To borrow a phrase, "God captains in the fight."

I am raising no question here as to why the universe is as it is. I take it as I find it. And in it I find this, that God is not content to let things go as they are, but he is forever at war with the evil that is in the world. Nothing heartens a man as does this faith. The final outcome is certain: Right some day must win. We are not following a forlorn hope: Christ shall put all his enemies under his feet. And in the battle we ourselves are workers together with God.

> "Say not the struggle naught availeth,
>   The labor and the wounds are vain,
> The enemy faints not, nor faileth,
>   And as things have been they remain.
>
> "If hopes were dupes, fears may be liars;
>   It may be, in yon smoke concealed,
> Your comrades chase e'en now the fliers,
>   And, but for you, possess the field."

(3) And this leads me to say a third thing: The method of the cross is the method we must follow if

we would do our part in delivering men from sin and all its evil train.

As Christ dealt with sin, so must we deal with it. The cross of Christ in history is the revelation before our eyes of the method of the immanent God through the eternal ages. And God's method must be our method also. When at Cæsarea Philippi Peter confessed Jesus to be the Christ, and Jesus had begun to teach his disciples that the law of the cross would certainly lead to his crucifixion, Peter made bold to take hold of him and to rebuke him. But Jesus very sternly rebuked Peter, saying, "Get thee behind me, Satan; for thou mindest not the things of God, but the things of men." Or as Glover translates it, "You think like men, and not like God." Or to give Moffatt's translation, "Your outlook is not God's, but man's." God thinks in terms of sacrifice. God's outlook is in the direction of service through suffering. "Without the shedding of blood there is no remission of sins." Therefore does Jesus lay down the supreme law of discipleship: "If any man would come after me, let him deny himself, and take up his cross, and follow me."

And only as we identify ourselves with men who sin and suffer, only as we share their sorrows, only as we bear their sins and sorrows in our own souls, shall we be able to bear them away. Under this sign we conquer. An impressive instance of the very thing that I have in mind took place recently in a little Southern city. A pastor's wife was in the hospital at

the point of death. A critical operation was necessary
to save her life. A blood transfusion was required if
she was to have strength to go through the operation.
The doctors could not make use of her husband's
blood. It was Sunday morning at the hour of worship. The minister was just about to administer the
Sacrament of the Lord's Supper, and the congregation to receive the tokens of the broken body and shed
blood of our Lord, when a note was read asking for
someone to volunteer to give his blood to save the life
of the pastor's wife. In an instant twenty-five strong
young men rose ready to go to the hospital. For them
Christ's blood had not been shed in vain! The significance of the atoning sacrifice was never more beau-
tifully illustrated. And just so with reference to sin
and sorrow: We must bear them ourselves if we
would bear them away.

II

We have been speaking of the cross of Christ in
its relation to the forgiveness of sins. Let us make
sure that we understand what the words really mean,
those familiar words, "the forgiveness of sins."

When we stand with the congregation and repeat
the words of the ancient creed, "I believe in the forgiveness of sins," exactly what are we saying? What
is the meaning of the forgiveness of sins? The
Apostle Paul and other New Testament writers having been brought up under a system in which religion
was looked upon as a matter of obedience to law,

even after they had broken away from that system, were under the necessity of using the language that was best understood among the people to whom they wrote. With us the theory of the atonement that has most shaped our thinking has been that presented in Anselm's great work, *Cur Deus Homo?* Now Anselm's theory was formulated when the most exact thinking was done in the terminology of Roman jurisprudence. And I have been apprehensive all along that when I have spoken of "the forgiveness of sins" it might be taken for granted that I was speaking in terms of the law courts or that others might be misinterpreting me by themselves thinking in law terms. Let me say then at once that I am not thinking in terms of law but in terms of life. "Forgiveness" is an intensely personal word; it has to do with persons, not with courts and law. Just as the suffering of Christ must be thought of personally, as God's personal way of dealing with sinners, so must the forgiveness of sins be understood. And to be understood it must be experienced. Without the experience of the divine forgiveness the theologian need no more undertake to talk about it than a blind man to describe the rainbow or a deaf man to speak of a sonata.

(1) By the forgiveness of sins we mean the restoration of personal relations between God and man.

Sin separates man from God—drives him out of Eden, sends him into the far country. Now man was made for fellowship with God. Apart from God and away from him, no man ever fully comes to himself. For sin creates immeasurable distances between man and God. Man's deepest need is fellowship with God. Without God man is lonely and forsaken. Now what the forgiveness of sins does for a man is this: it welcomes the prodigal back home again; it unlocks the gates of paradise and lets in the fallen Adam once more. It is as when a friend takes back to love and confidence a friend who has offended; it is as when a mother wipes the tears from the eyes of her disobedient and now repentant child; it is as when the father puts the kiss of forgiveness upon the cheek of his son, lost but now found again, dead, but now alive to a father's love. This is the experience that the Apostle Paul was giving expression to when he said: "Because ye are sons, God sent forth the Spirit of his Son into our hearts, crying Abba, Father." And "Abba," it will be remembered, is just that dear home-word for "father" that Paul had used when a child. The closeness of his filial relation to God the Father required him to make use of that close and intimate word of childhood and home.

And we see now at once how the death of Christ is related to such an experience as this. Nothing that we can possibly imagine could more certainly lead to restoration of personal relations than God in Christ coming all the way to the cross to save men. And God, let it be emphasized, takes the initiative. It is not man who first turns toward God; it is rather the divine Father who turns first toward man. It is the seeking, suffering God that reaches the heart of man.

If we look back upon our lives there are sins we have been guilty of which, when we brood over them, take all the joy and confidence out of life. But the testimony of the saints in all centuries is that the forgiveness of sins lifts from the conscience the load of guilt and enables one to go forth and face the whole world with confidence and joy. It is the language of personal experience that shouts in Paul's words: "Being justified by faith, we have peace with God through our Lord Jesus Christ; through whom also we have had our access by faith into this grace wherein we stand; and we rejoice in hope of the glory of God." Pause a moment and look at the great new Christian words in the passage just quoted. Here they are: "peace," "faith," "grace," "joy," "hope"! Here are the characteristic Christian ideas. And, as Dean Inge says, "when these words threaten to drop out of our vocabulary, or are used with an unpleasant suspicion of unreality, cant, or affectation, we may be sure that we are losing the essence of the Christian spirit, and are falling back into paganism."

It is the realization of the fact that the suffering and seeking Father has in Christ gone to the cross for our salvation that calms our fears and enables us to stand and rejoice in hope of the glory of God. In the presence of that amazing fact what have we to fear?

(2) Let this also be said: The forgiveness of sins brings about the integration and reconstruction of the moral personality.

The astonishing thing about the New Testament —I had almost said, the most astonishing thing—is that Christianity knows no hopeless cases! Take, for instance, the story which the Early Church would not let die and has preserved for us in the eighth chapter of the Fourth Gospel, the story of the woman taken in the very act of adultery. To her Jesus said, "Neither do I condemn thee; go thy way; from henceforth sin no more." Read the account of Zacchæus the publican, the man who had sold his self-respect for money. Jesus went home with him, called him a son of Abraham, and laid down his principle of dealing with erring men—"The Son of Man came to seek and to save that which was lost." Read again the Acts of the Apostles and the letters written by Paul. In these we find the story of the triumph of Christ over sin and sorrow—the most wonderful story ever told. No wonder Paul exclaims, "Thanks be to God who always leadeth us in triumph in Christ." The Early Church was without doubt made up largely of "a ludicrous collection of trivial people, very ignorant and very common; fishermen and publicans, as the Gospels show us, 'the baker and the fuller,' as Celsus said with a sneer." Yes, but Christ conquered them, and they "washed their robes and made them white in the blood of the Lamb." And from those first days of the triumph of the gospel down to the present

hour the history of the real progress of Christianity
has been the spiritual biography of men and women,

". . . who have mightily won
God out of knowledge and good out of infinite pain,
And sight out of blindness and purity out of a stain."

But if the time ever comes when the Church is
little more than an association of highly respectable
people, no matter how worthy may be the end that
brings them together, then the Church will take its
place along with scores of other institutions having
a very decent place in society but no redeeming mis-
sion among men. The main business of the Church is
to proclaim the good news of salvation to those who
are without hope—or say rather whose only hope is
in the love of God as manifested in the cross of Christ.

We have been speaking about sin and the divine
forgiveness. But we may be told that nobody is worry-
ing about sin any more, and, therefore, nobody is
concerned about the divine forgiveness. Walt Whit-
man's paganism seems to be characteristic of our
times:

"I think I could turn and live with animals, they are
　　so placid and self-contained.
I stand and look at them sometimes an hour at a
　　stretch.
They do not sweat and whine about their condi-
　　tion,

They do not lie awake in the dark and weep for their
   sins,
They do not make me sick discussing their duty to
   God."

But I am not so sure about this. Indeed, I do not
believe that it truly represents the spirit of the times
we live in. It may be that old theological terms have
fallen into disuse. It may be that we have learned
how to keep our sorrows to ourselves. We do not
talk so much nowadays about *sin* as an abstraction,
but we do know *sins* as concrete realities. There are,
it is true, many things that call us away from thoughts
about ourselves. The world was never more alluring
than it is now. There are so many bright things to
interest and occupy us. The lust of the flesh, the lust
of the eyes, and the pride of life were never quite so
attractive. And the materialistic psychology which
has been popularized through books and magazines
is all on the side of the senses. But the human heart
is incurably human; the soul still perishes without
God. Man remains orphaned and alone without the
Heavenly Father. The tragedy of many an empty life
finds expression in the lines of Fanny Heaslip Lea:

"She made a little shadow-hidden grave
   The day Faith died;
Therein she laid it, heard the clod's sick fall,
   And smiled aside—
'If less I ask,' tear-blind, she mocked, 'I may
   Be less denied.'

"She set a rose to blossom in her hair,
    The day Faith died—
'Now glad,' she said, 'and free, at last, I go
    And life is wide.'
But through long nights she stared into the dark
    And knew she lied."[6]

The language of Augustine is forever true. "O God, thou hast made us for thyself and the human heart is restless till it rests in thee." We lie when we pretend to be satisfied without God. We lie when we seem to be content with our sins. And never more than now have souls been desolate, and lives empty, and hearts sad. The tragedies that every morning's paper calls to our notice bear witness to this fact. We do not need to go beyond the circle of our own acquaintance to see the ruin sin is working in individual lives and in human society. The ancient judgment stands confirmed: "There is no distinction; for all have sinned and fall short of the glory of God."

Now nothing answers the cry of the soul as does the cross of Christ. Here deep calleth to deep—the deep of God's mercy to the deep of man's need. In the presence of the cross we exclaim, "When thou saidst, Seek ye my face; my heart said unto thee, Thy face, Lord, will I seek." Here we find the self-authenticating Christian gospel. To the sins and sorrows of men the cross speaks with final and divine authority. "And I, if I be lifted up from the earth, will draw all men unto myself" is both prophecy and history.

---

[6]Quoted with the author's permission.

For wherever Christ on the cross is lifted up before men their hearts have with unfailing certainty turned toward him. Nothing attracts as does the magnet of the cross. And this is not a theory to be defended; it is a fact to be proclaimed. It is not a proposition that needs argumentation; it is an experience that calls for affirmation. There can be no question that too many of our Modernists have been too much concerned over "the work of explanation" and not enough concerned about "the work of salvation." Do not misunderstand me: the work of explanation must be done; no man should hesitate to follow the truth out to the utmost edge of reality. But with the preacher, the love of men comes before the love of truth, and it may turn out that the pragmatic principle is worth considering; if a thing works it must be true. It is always the truth in a doctrine that saves —never the error that is in it. And the gospel of Christ and his cross remains through all the generations "the power of God unto salvation to everyone that believeth."

III

No story ever told has had such power to touch the hearts of all sorts and conditions of men. It authenticates itself.

James Denney bears witness to the authority of the cross in the following words:

"The doctrine of an atonement for sins, made in Christ's death, has never been accepted in the Church

simply as the speculation of three accidentally privileged men—Peter, Paul, and John. The authority it
enjoys and has enjoyed from the beginning of time is
due to this, that the Holy Spirit has borne witness by
and with that doctrine in men's hearts, making them
sure that in accepting Christ's death thus interpreted,
they are accepting the very soul of God's redeeming
love. If there is one truth in the whole Bible which
is covered by the *Testimonium internum Spiritus
sancti,* and by the consenting witness of Christians in
all ages, it is this. It has an authority in it or along
with it by which it vindicates itself to faith as divinely
and infallibly true; it asserts itself irresistibly, and
beyond a doubt, as the supreme revelation of God's
judgment and mercy to penitent souls. There can be
no authority higher than that."[7]

One of the older missionaries from India tells
how one day a pundit from the hills said to him, "Get
out of this country and quit telling that story of the
cross. We have many religions and many stories of
the gods, but no such story as the story of the cross.
And if you do not stop telling that story, the people
will forsake their religion and go to following Jesus."
So mightily does the message of the cross appeal to
men who are morally in earnest.

Sometime ago *The Christian Century* carried an
interesting and illuminating story. I omit the names.
In a city of one of the Central States the pastor of
the First Unitarian Church had been giving a series
of sermons on the life of Christ. As the Lenten season

---

[7] *Studies in Theology,* pp. 222-223.

drew toward its close there came the place for a sermon on the crucifixion, and the pastor had announced that on the next Sunday he would preach on: "The Man on Trial for His Life: His Crucifixion." But when the congregation gathered for the service the bulletin of the church announced an entirely different subject. And with this change in subject appeared this note written by the minister: "As I read and reread the accounts given in the Gospels, I found myself too profoundly stirred to attempt the translation of thought and feeling into speech. The denial by Peter; the trial before the High Priest, Herod and Pilate; the mocking and the cruel scourging; and finally the terrible anguish and death of the Man upon the cross; all are so greatly moving in their tragedy that I felt if I trusted myself to speech, I should be completely overcome." *The Christian Century* adds this comment: "What would happen if even church people should learn to read the story of Jesus with their emotions as well as with their ordinary mental apparatus?" And may I add this further comment: What would happen if preachers in the evangelical churches should pause for a time from preaching about the events of the day and bring from Sunday to Sunday some message about the Eternal Christ? What would happen if with hearts suffused with gratitude divine they should again and again undertake to show how here in the story of the anguish and death of the Man upon the cross is an exhibition before men and angels of the suffering love that is eternal in the heart of God? Bishop Eugene Russell Hendrix used to tell of a young minister who found one morning on his pulpit a note reading as follows: "Sir, we would see Jesus." He accepted the rebuke and began to preach the gospel of Christ and him crucified. Then again he found another note on his pulpit which was in the following language, "Then were the disciples glad when they saw the Lord." Nothing speaks to the human heart as does the preaching of the cross.

Distant and cold are our best logical forms and theological statements when they attempt to set forth the meaning of the cross. They are all open to criticism, and they all fail to satisfy the preacher that writes them down. But the cross on Calvary does speak home to the guilty conscience and the contrite heart in a language all its own. It is the very "word of God," the *language God uses,* to carry his message home. We may be puzzled over it when working in the study or sitting in the lecture room. But it all seems so plain when we are in our closet on our knees, or when kneeling at the Lord's table we hear the words spoken, "The body of our Lord Jesus Christ, which was given for thee. . . . The blood of our Lord Jesus Christ, which was shed for thee."

It speaks to us as does great music or great art or great poetry. It is more significant than all the symbols and more sacramental than all the sacraments. In it the Spirit of God whispers forgiveness and peace and life eternal.

It has been said that no rallying cry ever appealed to men as does the call, "Come and suffer with us." This is the call of God to men from the cross. Come and see where is to be found the sin and sorrow of the world. Come and sit down by the suffering and take their burdens on your heart. Come and get under the weight of the world's sin until you feel the shame and guilt of it to be your own. Come and seek out the causes of the evils in human society and dedicate your life to the building of a better world. Come share in the work of the world's Redeemer. Take up your cross and follow Christ. In your own flesh and soul, fill up on your own part "that which is lacking of the afflictions of Christ" for the sake of saving men and women and little children from sin and sorrow, and you will enter into "the fellowship of his sufferings" and experience the highest joy that comes to man, the joy that seeketh us through pain.

> "O Cross that liftest up my head,
>   I dare not ask to fly from thee;
> I lay in dust life's glory dead,
> And from the ground there blossoms red
>   Life that shall endless be."

VII

THE AUTHORITY OF THE CHURCH

"O God, the Father of our Lord Jesus Christ, our only Saviour, the Prince of Peace; give us grace seriously to lay to heart the great dangers we are in by our unhappy divisions. Take away all hatred and prejudice, and whatsoever else may hinder us from godly union and concord; that as there is but one body and one Spirit, and one hope of our calling, one Lord, one faith, one baptism, one God and Father of us all, so we may be all of one heart and one soul, united in one holy bond of truth and peace, of faith and charity, and may with one mind and one mouth glorify Thee, through Jesus Christ our Lord. Amen."—THE BOOK OF COMMON PRAYER.

VII

THE AUTHORITY OF THE CHURCH

According to the Catholic view of Christianity the Church has authority to require an explicit and implicit obedience which includes within its range the intellect as well as the conscience, things to be believed as well as things to be done. The Plenary Catechism puts it thus: "The Church cannot err when it teaches a doctrine of faith or morals. A doctrine of faith or morals refers to whatever we must believe and do in order to be saved."

Also, the Church has authority to forgive sin. The Church is looked upon as *a saving personality complete in itself,* possessing a corporate mind and conscience, and able to function organically in independence of the moral life of its officials. As the famous Bishop of Carthage wrote: "No man can have God for his father who does not have the Church for his mother. From her womb we are born, by her milk we are nourished, by her spirit we are made alive."

It is quite easy for us who look upon this view of the Church as mythical and unspiritual and highly harmful to intellectual and religious life, to swing far to the other extreme and fail to see how central a place the Church does hold in the thought and life of the New Testament. And it is quite important that we should realize that evangelical Christianity is in grave danger at the present time through a failure to understand and appreciate the true place and function of the Church in human society. There is an authority that inheres in the Church, and this authority is not less significant, but rather more meaningful, that it is found to be not external but inward, not mechanical but spiritual, not ecclesiastical but personal.

Few things would go farther just at the present time in the direction of the building up of the Kingdom of God and the drawing together in closer spiritual unity of all the branches of the Church than would the recovery of the apostolic doctrine of the Church of Jesus Christ. It is indeed utterly vain to attempt to trace back to Jesus any one of the churches we now find in the world claiming divine authority and origin. But Jesus did gather about him the twelve apostles and other followers; they did baptize in his name; he did institute the Supper of the Lord; and after his ascension his disciples did straightway begin to organize churches. The New Testament writers do attach great value to the Church as central in the divine plan for the evangelization of the world. As a distinguished lecturer on the Lyman Beecher Foundation said some years ago: "History proves that the continuance of Christianity is dependent upon the Church. . . . Whenever the Church prospers, society improves. Whenever the Church languishes, society degenerates. When the Church is vigorous, the social atmosphere becomes bracing and clear; when the Church becomes worldly and corrupt, the sun is turned into darkness and the moon into blood. . . . There is no hope for the triumph of the Christian religion outside the Church."[1]

In answering the question, Where lies the authority of the Church of Jesus Christ? We reply in three important statements:

First, the authority of the Church is in "the power of the keys," that is to say, the right and privilege of men and women who have themselves been forgiven and brought into personal relation to Christ, to forgive the sins of the erring and to open the door to the Kingdom of God to all who truly believe.

Secondly, the authority of the Church lies in its God-given prerogative of applying the truths of Christianity to the society we live in, and thus to bring in the establishment of the Kingdom of God on earth, that is to say, the reign of God in the institutions of our civilization.

Thirdly, the authority of the Church is found in its consistent and united testimony through the centuries to the essential things of the Christian faith, the *communis consensus fidelium*. This authority continues in the Church of the Twentieth Century as a living witness to an abiding reality.

The present lecture will be given to the discussion of these three propositions.

---

[1]Charles E. Jefferson in *The Building of the Church*.

And, in order that there may be no possibility of misunderstanding the position here taken, let it be once and for all understood that *we are not speaking of the Church as an ecclesiasticism functioning organically, but of the whole body of Christ's followers acting as individuals but in fellowship one with another.*

I

The Church is to carry on her work and to exercise her authority by following the method of Jesus, the method of the cross. The cross of Christ is God's message of forgiveness and his method of salvation.

The authority of the Church, then, is in the right and privilege of men and women themselves forgiven and in fellowship with Christ, to forgive the sins of men and lead them to a forgiving Saviour.

When we repeat the words of the ancient creed, "I believe in the forgiveness of sins," do we mean thereby only to say that we believe that God has provided a way whereby sins may be forgiven? and do we stop there? We must go farther than that. When we repeat that confession of faith we should also mean that *we believe we Christians are to forgive* those who have sinned. I find that Bishop Temple holds this same view. I quote:

"When one says that he believes in the forgiveness of sins, he ought not to mean that he holds the opinion that God forgives sins, but that he believes in forgiving sins as a principle of practical life—God's life and man's. He puts trust in God's forgiving love; but trusting that as good, he must needs imitate it; and therefore he trusts also the excellence and power of forgiveness in human affairs."[2]

With reference to those who have sinned against God and whose conscience cries out in alarm, the Church as an institution has no authority to announce the divine forgiveness of sins. Forgiveness is personal; it is the bringing back of lost friendship. It is restoration of fellowship with the Father. God does not delegate that prerogative to another. A secondhand and official forgiveness is not what the human soul needs. The soul needs God. In forgiveness God gives himself. No man, therefore, nor any delegated authority, can stand between the penitent sinner and his God. But it *is* the duty and sublime privilege of the Church to preach Jesus Christ and him crucified, and to announce to all broken and contrite hearts that God stands ready to pardon and deliver from all our sins.

"I believe in the forgiveness of sins." There is no article in the creed more precious to sinners than this announcement of the glad tidings of the divine forgiveness.

It is almost impossible to overstate the importance and place of forgiveness in the Christian community. And yet somehow its place in the New Testament has been to a large degree overlooked. Turn then to the Gospels and read.

---

[2]*Christ the Truth*, p. 318.

We begin with the Lord's Prayer, the Disciple's Prayer for the Coming of the Kingdom: "Forgive us our debts, as we also have forgiven our debtors." The forgiveness of those who have trespassed against us is already an accomplished fact with the disciple when he prays, "Forgive us our debts." Read the Beatitudes: "Blessed are the merciful, for they shall obtain mercy." Now mercy should be defined as *compassion and forgiveness displayed toward a sinner*. And now for the sake of its impressiveness permit me to give a passage from Dr. Moffatt's *Everyman's Life of Jesus:*

"If you forgive men their trespasses,
    then your heavenly Father will forgive you;
    but if you do not forgive men,
  your heavenly Father will not forgive your tres-
        passes either."

"If your brother sins, check him, and if he repents, forgive him." Then Peter came up and said to him, "Lord, how often is my brother to sin against me and be forgiven? Up to seven times?" Jesus said to him, "Seven times? I say, seventy times seven! That is why the Realm of heaven may be compared to a king who resolved to settle accounts with his servants. When he began the settlement, a debtor was brought in who owed him three million pounds; as he was unable to pay, his master ordered him to be sold, along with his wife and children and all he had, in payment of the sum. So the servant fell down and prayed him 'Have patience with me, and I will pay you it all.' And out of pity for that servant his master released him and discharged his debt. But as that servant went away, he met one of his fellow-servants who owed him twenty pounds; and seizing him by the throat he said, 'Pay your debt.' So his fellow-servant fell down and implored him, saying, 'Have patience with me, and I will pay you.' But he refused; he went and had him thrown into prison, till he should pay the debt. Now when his fellow-servants saw what had happened they were greatly distressed, and they went and explained to their master all that had happened. Then the master summoned him and said, 'You scoundrel of a servant! I discharged all that debt for you, because you implored me. Ought you not to have had mercy on your fellow-servant, as I had on you?' And in hot anger his master handed him over to the torturers, till he should pay him all the debt. My heavenly Father will do the same to you unless you each forgive your brother from the heart."

The New Testament Church understood this teaching. We find it all through the writings of the apostles. Paul writes to the Romans: "If thine enemy hunger, feed him: if he thirst, give him drink; for in so doing thou shalt heap coals of fire upon his head. Be not overcome of evil, but overcome evil with good." And John writes: "My little children, these write I unto you that ye may not sin. And if any man sin, we have an Advocate with the Father, Jesus Christ the righteous." Mark well those words, "If any man sin, *we* have an Advocate with the Father." Not the man alone who had sinned has an Advocate. Of course *that*—but much more. Rather, "We" —the members of the Christian fellowship—*"We* have an Advocate with the Father." His sin is our shame. The sinner hurts the entire group of Christians. When one member suffers all suffer. Therefore, the whole Christian fellowship makes *his* case *their* case before the Advocate with the Father. This is New Testament Christianity. This is the Christianity that we need to practice in this Twentieth Century. There is no swifter way to bring in the coming of the kingdom than to practice the gospel of forgiveness.

And in this connection it cannot be forgotten that when Christ was being crucified, when the nails were piercing his hands and feet, he prayed, "Father, forgive them; for they know not what they do." Nor does any man know the full consequences of his sins. If he did he would not commit them; and certainly if we knew the full fruitage of his wrongdoing in damage to himself alone, we should stand ready to forgive and by forgiving to bring salvation to him. This indeed is the message of the cross: "Father, forgive them, for they know not what they do."

Now these are several reasons why, as Christians, we must practice the gospel of forgiveness.

1. We cannot have fellowship with the forgiving God if we do not from the heart forgive our offending brothers.

We have seen that the divine forgiveness of sins is not a legal transaction. Rather it is personal. It is the restoration of personal relations between the erring child and his Father. But God is love—self-forgetful, self-sacrificing, and forgiving love. The unforgiving soul can have no fellowship with the forgiving God. The Christian, therefore, always stands in the spirit and attitude of *"forgivingness."*

Let me submit the following as a definition of the Christian Church: *The Christian Church is the society of the forgiven and forgiving.* Through Christ Christians have been forgiven, and like Christ they stand always ready to forgive. "The forgiven and forgiving," so may we ever be!

2. And we must practice the gospel of forgiveness because there is redeeming power in forgiveness, in human forgiveness as well as in divine forgiveness. I say the power of redemption is in the act and attitude of forgiveness on the part of Christlike men toward sinners.

See how much is implied in human forgiveness and how it operates to save men from their sins:

(1) *It shows them that we still believe in them.*

Forgiveness reveals to others that we have faith in their power to rise and be themselves again. George Adam Smith, in his beautiful sermon on "The Forgiveness of Sins," has pointed out that the divine forgiveness of sins is just God's new trust in the soul he has forgiven. So God trusted Abraham. So Jesus trusted the sinful women and said, "Go, and sin no more." So the Risen Christ trusted Simon Peter and committed to him the interests of his kingdom.

Now, it is good to be trusted. Nothing so lifts a man out of himself as to feel and know that he is trusted by good men. Character withers in an atmosphere of suspicion. The finest graces of the soul come to full bloom in the warm atmosphere of trust and confidence.

(2) When we exercise the grace of forgiveness, *we declare to others that we actually believe in the forgiving and saving power of God.*

We trust little because we believe little. We lose faith in men because we have lost faith in God. When we actually proceed to shape our conduct upon the faith that all men are redeemable and that Christ knows no hopeless cases, then we inspire others to believe our gospel. Faith in God is contagious. It passes from ourselves to others.

As everyone knows, the great evangelist of the Eighteenth Century was John Wesley. His conduct inspired faith in those who had no faith. Men believed in themselves because Wesley believed in God. Nothing is more characteristic of that great evangelist than his belief in men, his trust that by the power of God men could rise into newness of life. Some men deceived him, some disappointed him. His critics think him sometimes trustful far beyond the bounds of wisdom. But his faith in men was justified. I give here a letter written by Wesley. This will show better than anything I can say the quality of his faith.

William Shent, a Leeds barber, had become a Methodist itinerant. But after several years of useful service he had fallen into grievous sin, and had been summarily expelled from the society of Methodists. When John Wesley heard of it he wrote this letter to the Methodist Society in Keighley:

"I have a few questions, which I desire may be proposed to the society at Keighley.

"Who was the occasion of the Methodist preacher's first setting foot in Leeds? William Shent.

"Who received John Nelson in his house at his first coming thither? William Shent.

"Who was it that invited me, and received me when I came? William Shent.

"Who was it that stood by me when I preached in the street, with stones flying on every side? William Shent.

"Who was it that bore the storm of persecution for the whole town, and stemmed it at the peril of his own life? William Shent.

"Whose word did God bless for many years in an eminent manner? William Shent's.

"By whom were many children now in Paradise begotten in the Lord, and many now alive? William Shent.

"Who is he that is ready now to be broken up and turned into the street? William Shent.

"And does nobody care for this? William Shent fell into sin, and was publicly expelled from the society; but must he be also starved? Must he with his gray hairs and all his children be without a place to lay his head? Can you suffer this? O, tell it not in Gath! Where is gratitude? Where is compassion? Where is Christianity? Where is humanity? Where is concern for the cause of God? Who is a wise man among you? Who is concerned for the Gospel? Who has put on bowels of mercy? Let him arise and exert himself in this matter. You here all arise as one man, and roll away the reproach. Let us set him on his feet once more. It may save both him and his family. But what we do, let it be done quickly.

"I am, dear brethren, your affectionate brother."

And who can doubt the saving power of such forgiveness. It makes the fallen brother feel that he is once more fully trusted; it restores him again to the society of the Christian brotherhood; it reveals to him the compassionate heart of the divine Father waiting to forgive and to save. It speaks the restoring word, *Return and sin no more*.

3. But there is something more to be said: Forgiveness is not an easy thing in man any more than it is in God. The cross is the measure of the cost of forgiveness. If we are truly to forgive we must surely endure the cross.

To forgive is not to smile and shake hands and say we will forget. To forgive is to associate oneself with the sinner and to sacrifice something with a view to bringing him back to righteousness, and in order to sweeten our own souls with reference to the offender.

Horace Bushnell was, with the older generation of preachers, a pathfinder in the realm of spiritual reality. His epoch-making work would have been easier if he had had in his hand the critical apparatus of the present-day theologian. But he followed his own heart and the leadings of God's Spirit, and there came to him the illuminated mind. He was always brooding over the doctrine of the Vicarious Sacrifice. He had already written the first volume of his great work on that highest of all themes, when the second and complementary volume was born. He describes the genesis of the new book as follows:

"I was writing a discourse on the inquiry, How shall a man be able to entirely and perfectly forgive his enemy, so as to forever sweeten the bitterness of his wounded feeling and leave no sense of personal revulsion? I was brought squarely down upon the discovery that nothing will ever accomplish the proposed real and true forgiveness, but to make cost in the endeavor, such cost as new-tempers and liquefies the reluctant nature. Why not say this of all moral natures, why not of the Great Propitiation itself?"

Yes, it did cost, it does cost God to forgive. The cross is his eternal heartache made manifest in time. And this is the method of redemption—God's method and ours also. Only as we make sacrifice of ourselves shall we save others. Nothing wins its way and saves as does suffering love. The method of the cross is the way of salvation. For us, it is not easy. Nor was it easy for him who fainted under the weight of the cross and died on it of a broken heart. At the heart of all true and redeeming forgiveness is a cross red with sacrificial blood.

Here, then, we find the true "power of the keys." To his disciples Jesus had said: "Whatsoever ye shall bind on earth shall be bound in heaven, and whatsoever ye shall loose on earth shall be loosed in heaven."

And in a very profound and spiritual sense this power of binding and loosing does inhere in the Christlike followers of Jesus. No man and no ecclesiasticism has any right to presume to take the place of God. But in the name of Christ we are privileged to say: "Almighty God, the Father of our Lord Jesus Christ, who desireth not the death of a sinner, but rather that he may turn from his wickedness and live, hath given power and commandment unto his ministers to declare and pronounce to his people, being penitent, the absolution and remission of their sins. He pardoneth and absolveth all those who truly repent and believe his holy Gospel."[3]

And we are privileged to go farther than that. When we laymen and ministers, believing fully in our gospel, trusting in the ability of sinful men to respond to the sacrificial approaches of love, and not doubting the willingness of the Father to go out and meet the returning prodigal, ourselves take the initiative and forgive men; that is to say, when we show that we stand in the attitude of forgiveness, then are we exercising the power of the keys, then are we making use of our authority to bind and loose, then are we opening the gates of new life to men. It was of this that the Apostle Paul was thinking when he wrote, "Brethren, even if a man be overtaken in any trespass, ye who are spiritual, restore such a one in the spirit of gentleness; looking to thyself, lest thou also be tempted. Bear ye one another's burdens,

---

[3]Book of Common Prayer.

and so fulfil the law of Christ." Such must be the attitude of the Church toward sinful individuals.

II

We raise now another question: What authority has the Church with reference to the world we live in with all its human institutions? We answer: The authority of the Church lies in its God-given prerogative of leading the way in the building of the Kingdom of God among men.

In general there are three attitudes that have been taken toward the world with its social and political institutions.

1. There is the attitude of aloofness, the position that the Church has nothing to do with these earthly things, that the gospel is designed to save individuals only.

We see something of this in the Church of the New Testament. The first Christians had, as a matter of course, fallen heir to Jewish apocalyptic, and it was extremely difficult for them to shake themselves free from that religion of despair. Jesus, it is clear, did transcend Jewish apocalyptic. But it was too much to expect that the disciples would soon do the same. Some of Paul's early utterances show that he himself had not yet outgrown the apocalyptic outlook. But all his work was planned on a different basis, all his campaigns for the evangelization of the world were planned as a wise general would plan for the conquest of the entire empire.

There is at the present time a school of critics who insist that in this particular Jesus was in perfect agreement with the Jewish apocalyptic outlook, that he was in fact looking toward the establishment of a kingdom with Jerusalem as its center, and that in the bringing in of this kingdom he looked for the forces of the other world visibly to coöperate. His ethics, therefore, are only *interim ethics*. He was, of course, disappointed in his hopes, and his teachings turn out to be entirely impracticable in this matter-of-fact world.

Well, we may say one thing about the position taken by these extreme critics—they have at least made it plain that the Jesus of the Gospels was no "pale Galilean." We are thankful for that much, while we decline to agree with these newer critics that Christianity, the sanest of all religions, traces back to a visionary and a fanatic.

Also, we have to-day a large group of earnest and sincere Christians, frightened by the trend of modern thought and in despair for the future of the world unless other than spiritual forces be brought into play, and they insist that the one concern of the Church should be to save as many individuals as possible so as to make up the number of the elect and be ready to meet the Lord in the air when he comes to claim his own. But this, I must insist, is a reversion to a lower type of religion and an abandonment of the program of Jesus.

There are others, by no means fanatical, whose

scholarship and piety cannot be doubted, who nevertheless take the position that the Church should remain detached and aloof from merely mundane affairs. They view as impossible the scheme to "Christianize the social order." The finest of them all, that grand old Christian scholar, Francis L. Patton, writes as follows: "Men speak of Christian work in terms of the community and not of the individual. They talk of Christianizing the social organism, instead of saving souls, when as a matter of fact it would be as easy to vaccinate the social organism as to Christianize it."[4] Well, as a matter of fact, we have just about succeeded in "vaccinating the social organism." Vaccination is no longer meeting with opposition; it is now pretty generally accepted as the scientific way of dealing with smallpox. And we do hope by and by to get the public at large to yield assent to the teachings of Jesus as the one way to save the social organism from the disease of sin.

2. There is another attitude toward the institutions of the social and political world that we must mention. In this view the political methods and agencies of this world are to be used in the interest of the Church.

The advocates of this view begin by identifying the "Church" with the "Kingdom of God," and this is as bad from the viewpoint of exegesis as it is in its practical consequences. For when the Church is understood to be one and the same with the Kingdom

---

[4] *Fundamental Christianity*, pp. 174, 175.

of God, then the Church soon begins to behave as do the kingdoms of this world.

3. But the Church does have a solemn duty to discharge with reference to society. The gospel does have power to save, not individuals alone, but the civilization in which they live. We do believe that Christ shall reign till he has put all his enemies under his feet —enemies in the social organism and enemies in the human heart.

Moreover, in our view the social aspects of the gospel and the individual application of the Christian message cannot be separated the one from the other. Men are not detached integers living apart from others and wholly in themselves. We are bound up together in one bundle of life. The individual exists in society and society exists in the individuals that compose it. The Kingdom of God is indeed a new order of society in which men serve God as Father and love their fellow men as brothers. The teachings of Jesus are to apply to all human institutions—the home, the shop, the mine, the mill, the bank. The principles of Jesus must control in all our affairs—national, interracial, and international. But mere reforms are not enough. Laws and international agreements are good as far as they go, but they do not go far enough. "Except a man be born again he cannot see the Kingdom of God." The Church of Jesus Christ is in the world to bring in the reign of Christ in human hearts as well as in human institutions. And it should never be overlooked that human institutions are of